RELIGION
—my story—
OF PEACE?

EMMA EROS

First published 2020 by Connor Court Publishing

Copyright © Emma Eros 2020

All Rights Reserved.

This book is copyright. Apart from any use permitted under the *Copyright Act (1968) Cth* and subsequent amendments, no part of this book may be reproduced, reprinted, taken in part or whole, nor stored in a retrieval system, nor transmitted by any means or process whatsoever without the prior consent of the publisher.

ISBN 978-1-922449-27-6

Connor Court Publishing Pty Ltd
PO BOX 7257
Redland Bay QLD 4165

www.connorcourtpublishing.com.au

AUTHOR'S DISCLAIMER: This book is neither a scholarly nor an academic work. It is based on my own experiences, personal observations, research and lessons from my upbringing. Great care has been taken in writing this book. Any typos or errors found are the result of human imperfection. The information this book contains reflects, in my opinion, the mainstream understanding of Islam as generally taught to children who are raised in conventional Muslim households. My intention in this book is to encourage people to take a moment away from the world of 'soundbites' and to try and understand each other's perspectives in a proper and respectful manner.

Front Cover Design: Ian James

Printed in Australia

TABLE OF CONTENTS

Foreword by Mark Latham 5

Introduction 7

1 Emma Eros: The Story So Far 9
   My Childhood: The Lifelong Lessons 9
   Why do I choose to be a Muslim? 21
   My Public Life 28

2 Islam: A Basic Overview 55
   What is Islam? 56
   When and how did Islam start? 62
   Differences in Islamic Sects and Teachings 65
   What does Islam mean for today's world? 66

3 Myths and Facts I: Islam and Politics 75
   Is the Separation of Church and State Possible in Islam? 76
   Does Islam condone violence and terrorism? 84
   Do suicide bombers really get 72 virgins in heaven? 92
   Sharia Law: What it is and what it's not 94
   Caliphate: Does Islam require a theocratic state? 96
   Does the Quran preach hate? 99
   Was Prophet Muhammad violent towards Jews and Christians? 105

4 Myths and Facts II: Islamic Social Practices 111
   Muslim Women: Are they equal? 112
   Forced conversions 122
   Female Genital Mutilation 126

Honour Killings 127
Taqiyah: Can Muslims lie? 129
Does Islam condone slavery? 131
Does Islam tolerate gays and lesbians? 133
Does Islam promote polygamy? 136
Hijab, Niqab and Burqa: What's Islamic and what isn't? 138
Can Muslim women initiate a divorce? 139
Is Apostasy Punishable by Death? 140

5   Guidance for Muslims in the West 143
    Australia, We Have a Problem 143
    Is assimilation the answer? 160
    Racism and Islamophobia: Are they actually real? 165
    Can Muslims be loyal to the West? 172
    Australia, We Have a Solution 176

Notes 182
Bibliography 188

FOREWORD

This book has been a long time coming. It's no exaggeration to say that ordinary Australians have some deep concerns and anxieties about both Islam and Muslim immigration.

However, this isn't because we're a nation of racists and bigots. Rather, it's because we've seen what's happened to our suburbs since opening our doors to mass migration from Islamic nations.

Asking leaders and scholars within Australia's Islamic community to explain the failures of integration often results in accusations of Islamophobia. Unfortunately, this means that the real issues remain unaddressed.

There are days when I think so many of us could be won over if we had proper answers from someone who gets Islam and Muslim societies as an insider, but also gets our concerns and where we're coming from at the same time.

Having come to know Emma over the past several years now, I can vouch that there could be no better person to address these deep concerns than her. In fact, it's about time we had an Australian of Muslim background step forward to share an insider's perspective.

We can't be blamed for thinking that Muslim societies are male-dominated and don't really encourage women to get ahead in life and play lead roles.

Nor can we be blamed for thinking that integrating into Australian society has been a real struggle for so many Muslims from migrant backgrounds.

Emma's life as a successful businesswoman, happily married to an Aussie bloke and a mother of two beautiful children challenges both these stereotypes in a single hit.

You may or may not agree with everything she has to say, but it is important that her views get out there in the public space. It's about time someone like her who gets both cultures stepped up and put some sense into this debate that's been long overdue.

Mark Latham, Sydney, Australia 2019.

INTRODUCTION

There's an old saying that goes, 'never judge a book by its cover'. Well, I tend to disagree. The only way to decide whether you want to read a book is by reading the cover and the title. Truth is, neither of these will necessarily tell you what the book is about in detail, but it will provide you with a brief overview. Ultimately, this information is what you must rely on when making a snap decision about whether to purchase the book or not.

With that in mind, I want to start by congratulating you on your decision to read this book. If you are wondering what this is all about, we're off to a good start. It means that you are the thinking type. This book requires no prior knowledge or expertise in this area for you to appreciate what it has to offer.

It is fair to assume that whoever opens a book with the title, *Religion of Peace? – My Story*, must possess a degree of concern about Islam or Muslims or both. And to be honest, currently, how could you not?

From the whacky statements coming from crazy Imams to terrorists blowing up nightclubs, hardly a day goes by when Islam and Muslims don't feature in disturbing news headlines. It is only human nature to question, and people do have the right to judge these occurrences and events.

But think about this: both China and India have more university campuses than the United States. Yet, campus massacres rarely occur in either of those countries. When have you heard news that a crazy person decides to kill a bunch of innocent civilians, and then kill themselves? By contrast, such tragic attacks do unfortunately occur on a far too regular a basis in the United States.

It would, then, be completely logical to assert that the United States has a problem with campus massacre shootings, but does that make it a problem intrinsic within American culture, society or its Constitution? I would say no; the Founding Fathers of America would not approve of the level of unsolicited gun violence that has come to permeate the mainstream culture of the country they fought for.

Along the same vein, it's completely logical to say that Islam has a terrorism problem, but does that make it a problem inherent within Islamic teachings, society or scripture? Would the founding figures of Islam, its Prophet and his companions approve of September 11 or the Bali Bombings? If you are curious about the answer, then you are reading the right book.

I want to point out that this book is not a scholarly work. This is a work based on my honest quest to find answers to the same questions that you are seeking. It is, also, based on where I've been, what I've learnt, and the conclusions I have drawn first-hand.

So, please kick-back and enjoy the read as I share with you the observations I've made as someone who has had the benefit of being raised in an Australian Muslim household in the 1980's and 1990's.

1

EMMA EROS
THE STORY SO FAR

My Childhood: The Lifelong Lessons

Everyone has a story. You, me, your next-door neighbour, all of us have a story. I'm not unique in that respect. So, should everyone write a book? No; not all stories are worth telling. Before we get into the nitty gritty, let me first explain to you why I think my story is worth telling. Be honest: when you think of a Muslim, you think of a terrorist. You feel bad about this because you know you're not a hater, but you seem unable to stop this automatic association. I want to reassure you - this is not your fault.

When you think of women in the Muslim world, you think of an oppressed female gender. The image that springs to mind may be the incident when Malala Yousafzai was shot in the head by the Taliban for trying to obtain an education. Or, you may recall the incident when Asia Bibi, a Christian woman, was sentenced to death for blasphemy and later acquitted.

I am both a Muslim and a woman. I am not a terrorist neither am I oppressed, and perhaps most importantly, I am not the only Muslim woman who is neither of these pre-conceived things.

The world's first degree-awarding university was established by a woman 1200 years ago in the Muslim world.

The last century saw a greater number of female Muslim founding mothers, Presidents and Prime Ministers. Females are taking on these roles in greater numbers in Muslim countries than they are in Western ones. Meanwhile, in America, they're still awaiting their first female President.

When we think of an Islamic country such as Pakistan, we think of its rigid blasphemy laws. Yet, there are seats reserved in Parliament for its Christian minorities. You won't normally hear these goodwill gestures mentioned, why? Because all we seem to hear about when Muslims are mentioned in the media is terrorism and violence. So, the question actually becomes: why do I see Muslims and the world they come from in a different light?

Let me tell you, it isn't because I'm particularly educated on the subject. In reality, it's because I've lived as a Muslim and a woman, I grew up in a Muslim household, and I've come to realise the positive message about the fair and proper role of women in Islam isn't being heard loud enough. There's a fair chance that when you read the last few paragraphs, you may have reacted with a quiet 'wow' in your mind after discovering a Muslim woman started the world's first university.

This information is not hidden nor kept secret. It's information that can be discovered with a quick Google or Wikipedia search. And still, many people are simply not aware of it. This lack of information plays a part in fuelling misconceptions surrounding Islam and Muslims. It's also why I felt my journey is worth sharing. I want to take you on that journey back through time with me, into my past so you can see for yourself what it was like to grow up as a Muslim girl into adulthood, a Muslim girl who was very, very proud to be an Australian — and continues to be so to this day.

This is my journey. I lost my father before I was three years old, but I never saw myself as a victim. Rather it made me resourceful. I then utilised those entrepreneurial skills and created a successful businesswoman out of myself. I was able to achieve this without the help of anyone else.

Most importantly for the purpose of this book, is how the Islam I learnt in my family home has helped shape me into the strong, successful person I am today — against all the odds.

I was born in Australia to Lebanese migrants. I grew up in Sydney's outer western suburb of Lakemba. If stereotypes mean anything, then you're probably not surprised to learn that fact. At that time, many Lebanese migrants, just like my own parents, had decided to call Australia home. The area we settled in was beautiful, peaceful and trees lined our streets. It was a quiet, clean area to grow up in. Sadly, the same cannot be said today.

There were people of all age groups and cultural backgrounds living together in our area. We were all able to live in harmony together. Multiculturalism truly worked back in the days of my youth and you may wonder, how I reached that conclusion? Aside from personal experience, I arrived at this conclusion through two observations. The first one being: there was no terrorism in Australia at the time. And secondly, the number of migrants coming into Australia at that time was comparatively low. Together, these two factors made immigration appear manageable while migration wasn't 'in your face' to the average Australian.

Believe it or not, integration into Australian society was also not the exception, but the rule. Most Lebanese families maintained a harmonious balance between their culture inside their home and the culture out on the streets.

Of course, they retained some aspects of their cultural heritage - whether that was through teaching their language to their children, or the delicious dose of hummus and falafel that many Aussies have come to know and love today. By and large, they were loyal to this country. They were greatly appreciative of the opportunity they had been afforded to move to Australia and build a new, happy life here. They wanted to positively contribute to Australian society.

Driving through the streets of Sydney's outer western suburbs at this time, you couldn't help but notice the number of kebab shops, real estate agencies, travel agents and medical practices that were owned and operated by Lebanese migrant families.

Besides being Lebanese Australians, what did they all have in common with each other?

One word: entrepreneurship.

Yes, it's true that over time, some bad apples hailing from these communities have become a source of grief for modern Australia. But back then; anyone who had ever taken a drive up Haldon Street could see with their own eyes how hard these small business owners were working. You could see them contributing towards Australian society and its economy.

My father was no different. Neither was I to be honest. I hated being idle; I was a very self-reliant child from an early age. I've carried that with me into adulthood.

Whilst I was fortunate to come from an affluent family, I never took my parents' wealth for granted. I wanted to get out, start fulfilling my aspirations and fulfil my potential. So at a young age, I was offered my first job with McDonalds. Often other kids my age would be out and about playing on the streets, I instead chose to devote myself towards work and achieving my goals.

Honestly, most of my colleagues and clients never really asked what my ethnic background was. I didn't bring it into conversation. The truth was most people simply didn't care.

Sadly, this is no longer the case today. People have become much more curious, and while curiosity isn't always a bad thing, it can be irritating and saddening if that curiosity is stemming from a place of suspicion.

In any case, if there was one thing that my culture at home had emphasised on an almost daily basis, it was to respect your elders. Anyone that was older than you were essentially assumed to have seniority over you in terms of respect. So, if I boarded a public bus or train and I saw an elderly woman or man coming on board, I would always stand up and offer the elderly person my seat. If I saw an elderly person crossing the road, I would often accompany them to ensure they were able to cross safely. Superficial things such as race, religion, class, sect, creed or physical appearance never bothered me, and it wasn't something I took into account. I still hold these values today.

This was due primarily to Islam because Islam is the most colour-blind of all the faiths in the world. Islam does not care whether you are black, white, Arab, non-Arab or whatever. Muslims come from 57 different Muslim majority countries, separated by as many different flags, national anthems and passports; any division is not based on racial characteristics. Muslims come in all shapes and sizes, from white Bosnians to black Somalis, to brown Pakistanis and Arabs and every other shade in between.

My family taught me never to differentiate between anyone based on these factors. Sectarianism had no relevance or importance to us either. Did you know that among Lebanese communities, there are Maronites, Maron, Shiites and Sunnies among Lebanese Muslims? So even within our own community, which was only a subset of the wider Muslim community, there was a great deal of diversity surrounding us. And while we were Sunni Muslims, my family never looked down upon Maronite or Shiite Lebanese people as was so often the case in Muslim countries.

Overall, Australians are generally good people; they are warm-hearted, kind, friendly, easy to get along with and tolerant of differences. These undeniable values, which are imbued within Australian society, are never doubted. These same qualities and values, automatically assigned to non-Muslim Australians, and are not afforded to Muslim Australians. The general impression people seem to hold about Muslims is that we are a religion divided by sectarianism and ethnic violence. This never was and never has been my experience. As I said in my Introduction: all the school campus shooting massacres that we keep hearing about on a regular basis, these shootings are not representative of all individuals in American society.

It's the same with Muslims. We cannot all be defined as terrorists. Sometimes we may forget to cut other cultures the same slack that we cut ourselves. This isn't because we are a bunch of hypocrites! Rather, it's because we're all human.

Humans are imperfect.

Don't worry, many Muslims forget to do the same thing and forget to cut a little slack when judging Westerners in reverse. Each of us must ensure that we live up to the standards we have set for ourselves.

This was particularly important in our household. My mum sat down with me to talk about living up to my standards more times than I can possibly remember, and the content of those discussions could easily fill this book.

This accepting nature of a typical Muslim household showed through in many ways and took on many different forms. For instance, often when parents wanted to go out, they knew they could leave their children over at their next-door neighbour's place for babysitting. The neighbour who was babysitting us would treat us no differently than in the manner with which she treated her own children. And it goes without saying that the same offer of babysitting was reciprocated; whenever it was needed, they too left their children at our house at a moment's notice. People knew the value of reciprocity.

In our neighbourhood we had a very strong sense of community and trust. It was the kind of trust that we used to take for granted, but we now look back upon those days fondly as the "good old days". The general feeling today in a lot of communities and neighbourhoods is this community spirit and genuine trust is lacking. Worryingly, it seems to be disappearing at an ever-increasing rate.

These impromptu gatherings, minding of each other's children, stepping in when help was needed; this was the norm not the exception. And then, well, there was the food! That's always another great reason to gather, socialise and bond. What a delicious way it was to spend time with friends and neighbours. Neighbours and friends would all gather and bring food to share, adults enjoyed chatting whilst the children played. These gatherings filled with trust, bonding, openness and warmth are perhaps my strongest memories from my childhood. I remember the ease and enjoyment of coming together to share food, stories — and laugh.

We had many Indian friends in the neighbourhood too; the tandoori chicken they cooked was mouth-watering. Arab and Lebanese families such as my own would bring homemade kibbeh, hummus, falafel and many other traditional dishes. As the Middle Eastern cuisine is so rich in content and variety, it was never a struggle to impress your non-Arab next-door neighbour with a delicious banquet of shish taouks, vine leaves and baba ganoush.

Our enjoyment of sharing was as sweet as the baklava treats that followed the main course. The more we shared, the closer we became.

Often a birthday party in the park would become a neighbourhood event as all the families were invited to enjoy the celebration, regardless of how well the families knew each other. Not everyone who attended was Muslim and many of the Anglo-Celtic Australians in our neighbourhood loved coming to these gatherings and enjoyed mixing and socialising with the migrant families. In fact, they seemed to enjoy the foreign cuisine even more so than the migrant families themselves. Funny that.

My father worked for a company named James Hardy, a name that's now synonymous with the term asbestos. Unfortunately, my father worked for Hardy's and it was unknown to the general public, that asbestos caused cancer. My father was in his early thirties when he passed away from cancer. Before he died, my father returned to Lebanon, it was believed by mine and many other cultures that returning to your country of birth would miraculously cure you. Sadly, this was not the case for my father. He was laid to rest in Lebanon.

My parents immigrated to Australia when they were young to start over and build a new life and start a family. When my dad passed away, I was only two and a half years old and I do not have any recollections of him, only pictures to remember him by. We were very lucky that he left us in a financially comfortable situation. Everything I went on to achieve in life has been achieved by following in his footsteps as mum taught me to do. My father was a very sharp thinker and a hands-on person with a quick mind. I like to believe I am like my father. I like to think I possess similar qualities and traits that he had. He is missed a great deal and I deeply wish he could have been here to meet his grandchildren.

When I was growing up, my mum would often say, "If you're going to own a home, then make sure it's bought with your own money. Determination, hard work, save your money and prosperity will follow".

That attitude of self-reliance and responsibility for one's own self, was instilled into me by my mum. I suspect she developed these values due to losing my father at such an early age. Mum often spoke about the success of so many Muslim women throughout the pages of history that's inspired me to become the best and the brightest that I can be.

Remember I mentioned earlier about my first job at McDonalds? In my opinion, that is the spirit of true feminism, not this aggressive anti-man campaign that we see from the so-called third wave feminists today. I find them an affront to the spirit of true feminism, which should be about empowering women rather than promoting competition between men and women.

The extent to which we discussed my dad during my early childhood was limited. This was deliberately done for two reasons. The first was a religious reason, as Islam explicitly forbids friends and family from mourning the death of a loved one beyond the initial few days after the person's passing. Islam encourages people to be emotionally strong, to move forward with their lives and to look forward to the brightness that lies ahead, rather than dwelling on the darkness of the past. The other reason was more of a pragmatic one, the truth is, if you spend too much time dwelling about the person that is no longer there, you can become emotionally enveloped in sadness.

The grief over losing my father became almost paralysing, but perhaps my mum had always anticipated this. Mum knew what she was doing, and so every time dad was came brought up in conversation, it was done in a limited way, and I must say, they were quality times. This was because mum only ever spoke of the good memories and wonderful experiences that we had with our father. As we grew older, mum would tell us more about our family history and what our father was like as a person and regale us with stories about him. These are all fond memories, which I hold very close.

I can honestly say because I did not have any real memories of my father directly, I felt that I learnt to know my father because of the wonderful job my mother has done on ensuring we knew who he was as a person. It's as if she felt a responsibility in herself to pass on the knowledge that he had passed onto her. Mum taught us that Dad never liked being viewed as a victim because he wasn't a victim. Well, guess what? Nor do I like being viewed as a victim.

On one occasion, I distinctly recall that whilst at my Auntie's friends' home, I heard someone say, "be nice to that girl, she's just lost her father". I was stunned. I realise she was trying to ease my loss and didn't understand how her words could made me feel and I genuinely appreciate her kindness. But that moment made me realise how well-intentioned people who are trying to help after the loss of a loved one can inadvertently make you feel like a victim.

I had never asked for any sympathy. Neither did I expect it.

Another observation I've made of Arab and Muslim parents is that they seem to swing from one side of the pendulum to the other with regard to inculcating religious values to their children living in Western countries. At the one extreme you have the parents who tell their children that their Arab and Muslim identity supersedes their Australian identity - even though Australia is the country that houses them, feeds them, educates them and gives them a better opportunity in life than their countries of origin.

At the other extreme end of the spectrum, you have parents who seem to have no concern for their children and do nothing to discipline their children at all. The result ends up being that children often grow up feeling neither particularly Muslim nor particularly Australian. Of course, when they hit their teens, they can often develop an identity crisis as a result and all the ripple effects of that kick in. We see such children rejecting discipline at school, dropping out of school, taking drugs and generally not really being able to find a comfortable place for themselves within mainstream Australia. Why? Because they don't know which ethnic group or culture that they fit into. Identity is incredibly important to every individual. It delves into the very core of human nature, and it's this displacement that can make someone feel very isolated and lonely.

Thankfully, my mum, who was then a widow, fortunately did not swing from one side of the pendulum to the other. She maintained that balance excellently. I obviously wasn't very aware of this at the time; I was too little to wonder about such things. But, as I grew older and wiser, and then started a family of my own, I reflected upon my childhood and realised how well my mother had done in instilling that peace of mind in us.

I wasn't raised to be more of a Muslim than an Australian; I was not completely left to my own devices to develop an identity crisis. I've always thought that these moderate identities don't have to be mutually exclusive to Islam and Muslims. The Jews in the diaspora outside Israel are a great example.

It would be absurd, for instance, to ask Steven Spielberg whether he is more of an American than he is Jewish. It would be equally absurd, to ask whether he's more Jewish than American. The truth is, he is 'Jewish American' full stop. There is no contradiction in that. Where is it written that you cannot be both at the same time? In that same way, I am 'Australian Muslim' without contradiction. This balanced approach to my personal identity has been due largely to the combination of my mum's teachings, my own critical thinking and the inspiration that I found in Islam.

It must be said, that while Islam is a set of theological beliefs with its own ritualistic practices that you will no doubt read about in the next few chapters, there is another dimension to Islam that is rarely spoken about. I'm talking about the dimension that goes beyond theology and starts to straddle politics.

It is often this political dimension that's poorly represented not only by the media, but more importantly it is also poorly represented by the incompetent leadership of Muslim communities living in the West.

This is a subject that will be addressed at length in subsequent sections of my book.

For now, I hope that this section of my book has drawn your attention to the normality with which I as a Muslim girl grew up and took inspiration from Islam; the Islam as taught to me by my family. When the greater general population don't hear about this kind of normalcy, it becomes all too easy to watch the nightly news on the television or flick through the tabloids and assume that Islam must be a hateful religion. The public perception then drifts into one of violent, extremist, barbaric, hateful, divisive, and many other negatively associated mindsets.

In recent decades, just about every derogatory and judgemental word under the sun have come to be associated with Islam and Muslims. I'm the first to admit that some of that criticism is justified, but let's not blindly assume every single suspicion that we lay upon Muslims has a rational basis.

Many judgements are justified but let's not assume that we are perfect and that all our judgements are correct or final. As Australians we dislike being judged by others. If somebody were to imply all Australians were lazy, or that we're a nation of drunkards, then we would immediately take offence to being categorised with one broad swipe of the brush. We see the same train of thought regarding Catholicism, which, after recent news headlines, has become entangled with instances of paedophilia. All Muslims are not terrorists. Neither are all Catholics paedophiles. Both of those statements are true, regardless of the instant word associations.

We must try and engage our critical thinking skills when judging groups of people. All five fingers are not the same; this was another lesson my mum taught me.

So, the question the next inevitable question is: if Islam isn't the horrible religion so many people seem to think it is, and if multiculturalism isn't the horrible failure it's become today, "where did it go wrong"?

This is a fundamental theme that will be re-visited throughout this book as you work your way through subsequent sections and upcoming chapters. I hope that by the time you reach the last paragraph of the last chapter, some of the answers to the questions you may have had will have been answered or the answer seems clearer to you now.

Why do I choose to be a Muslim?

In the last section you learnt about the impact that Islam had on my childhood and upbringing. I grew up equally proud of both my national identity as an Australian, and my religious identity as a Muslim. At the same time, I didn't want to automatically be a Muslim simply because I was born one; I needed to be convinced it was the right path for me. Each of us is different, and it goes without saying we are all convinced and swayed by different modes of arguments, reasoning and provisions of proof.

In order for me to decide which religion I wanted to follow, I decided I felt it was important to conduct some research into all major religions. So I began to study religions such as Judaism, Christianity, Hinduism, Buddhism, Sikhism, as well as many other minor religions. I found that while the theology in these faiths could differ widely, the core moral teachings were remarkably similar. I could not find a religion that condoned, murder, rape or stealing, for instance. Every religion's central message was implicitly to help people find guidance and live a better life. I think it's because people often overcomplicate this simple message that we end up with the hatred we see in the world.

As for the big questions such as how we originated, what came before us, what happens after we die, these are fundamentally difficult questions that cannot be proven through experiment or hard evidence. What it really comes down to is belief, or what you might call a leap of faith. But this leap of faith can have a basis in reason, as indeed it should.

There are many unique and positive characteristics about Islam that we almost never hear about because we become so swept away with the negative side. Islam does not have a caste system, which puts one ethnic group above another. Everyone is seen as an equal and it is this wonderful practice of seeing everyone as equal that draws many people to Islam.

Islam literally only judges a person based on their character, nothing else. Islam teaches neither the poor to envy the rich, nor the rich to neglect the poor. It provides a just balance and framework to guide a society based on fairness. These values were not and still are not at odds with Australian values.

So, after I conducted my own investigation of Islam overall, I had genuine and sufficient reason to have that leap of faith. And now, here I am. That being said, we must never forget what each religion tries to do, which is to encourage its adherent to do good. Even if we disagree on core theologies, we can agree on what each religion intends to achieve.

The process of researching other religions and their beliefs was a thoroughly stimulating time in my life. I learnt a great deal from talking to adherents of different faiths; more than reading books ever taught me. As I said at the beginning, I am not a scholar and the basis of what forms this book is a combination of what I have learnt through firsthand observations and the direct feedback that I have received from others who also practice this faith.

As Islam sees itself as a continuation of Judaism and Christianity, it is not surprising that many of the Old and New Testament stories also feature in Islam. You'll find: Noah's Ark, Moses parting the Red Sea, King Solomon and the Temple, Jonah and the Belly of the Whale, Jesus and John the Baptist, and the list goes on. The Jewish word for God comes from the same origin as the Arabic word for God. Muslims worship the same God as the Jews and the Christians. These three religions are all from the same Abrahamic tradition.

Jews and Christians in the Middle East use the same term 'Allah' to refer to God. Allah is not a foreign god; he is meant to be the same deity as the Jewish-Christian god. The only difference is Jews and Muslims don't believe in the Trinity of Father, Son and Holy Spirit, only Christians do. The book of Genesis in the Old Testament, which both Jews and Christians also adhere to, refers to God as 'Elohim', which is from the same roots as 'Allah'.

Given this common synergy between Judaism, Christianity and Islam, I naturally fell in love with the Bible's collection of videos. There is a funny story to this because Islam, as you will see in the next section, is strongly opposed to idolatry. Some even consider the drawing of pictures, or the depiction of any living beings as a form of idolatry. Many ultra-orthodox Jews would share this view. This is the reason that there are no pictures of the Prophet Muhammad in Islam and it is also the reason why Muslims become so offended when others try to draw or depict him.

It is for this same reason that Muslims do not normally produce films or documentaries about their prophets or their lives. In their view, no film actor or actress could ever portray the prophets, especially not Muhammad, in a movie. It is equivalent to both blasphemy and idolatry. Although there have been a few such films and documentaries made, the public backlash in the Islamic world was costly enough to discourage any future attempts to make such movies.

Where did that leave curious little Emma when she was still at a young age? Well, I had no choice but to rely upon Jewish and Christian-made Biblical documentaries. Obviously, most Jews and Christians don't have a problem with Abraham, Isaac, Jacob, Moses, Aaron, or for that matter Jesus being depicted in film and television. While most of the stories were more or less the same, there are some minor differences between the way the Jewish, Christian and Islamic traditions convey these stories.

The younger version of me often became so immersed in those Biblical documentaries, that I'd forget that they were not produced by Muslim sources. It didn't really matter to me; the point was, I was able to see those religious stories in a visual form and those documentaries certainly did the trick.

I have been fortunate throughout my life to have had the opportunities to experience many friendships from a diverse group of communities, social cultures, religious cultures and ethnic groups. It's through being able to have many discussions with such a broad base of friends that I have come to learn more about other faiths than I could have learned from sitting in a library, reading a book. When you read a book, you're essentially interpreting the author's perspective through the written word. Their observations may well be valid, true and relevant but it's important to remember that everyone's experiences are different and may not align with your own worldview. It's through firsthand discussions with other people that we gain a great deal of insight into other cultures and beliefs. Having such a discussion may drastically change your viewpoint.

Therefore, I always say it's important to get out amongst society, have discussions, make your own observations and learn from those observations. No matter what a book may impart to you about a certain group of people, nothing can outweigh the value of learning and observing, through talking and listening. I will always be grateful to everyone I've spoken with for sharing their knowledge and experiences with me.

Books are no substitute for lived experiences, always try to remember that. I think maybe we all subconsciously know this, but we just don't actively remember it or keep it in the forefront of our mind. Imagine if you were to read two books, and each author presented a different perspective on a group of people. What would happen if one author stated that through her observations, she believed British people were arrogant, and a different author stated in her book that British people were very friendly and down to earth, which one would you be more likely to believe?

I can tell you now and with a great deal of certainty that it would not be the author that put forward view the most coherent and critically thought out point of views. Hardly anyone seems to care about the quality of reasoning or the evidence to support claims made in books. Academics may read them from a critical and coherent standpoint, but most of us don't. Most people simply believe at face value conclusions that match their own experiences in life. Many live in an echo chamber that re-enforces their own beliefs. Facebook is a perfect example of the echo chamber phenomenon, which prevents people having the ability to question their own set of beliefs or truly listen to the view of another.

So, if in previous experiences, you had found the British people to be arrogant, chances are that you will have a natural bias towards the author whose experiences align with your own. Likewise, if you had found British people to be friendly and down to earth, chances are, again, you will align naturally with this author whose experiences that you can relate to. This is how it works, nine times out of ten. So, when it comes to Muslims, the same principle should apply.

The difficulty nowadays appears to be the lack of personal engagement between the two communities. You would recall me mentioning earlier, how harmoniously people from all different walks of life were able to live alongside each other in the days of my youth. Now I've spoken about this at length, the remainder of my book is committed to discussing the reasons for how this turn around may have occurred.

A large part of this is down to global political events taking place overseas. This ends up having a trickledown effect on our society.

Sadly as a result, there are many mutual misunderstandings that not only exist on the part of mainstream Australian society, but equally so within Muslim communities. Australians tend to assume that the words Islam and Muslim are inextricably linked to the act of terrorism. Muslims also seem, to generally believe that Australians are racist and Islamophobic. As I am both Australian and Muslim, I understand both side's misconceptions about the other and how these misconceptions may have come about.

I'm not taking sides on this issue, rather, simply stating what I know to be true. To take sides would be to say that one party's grievances or misconceptions about the other aren't valid. I am, in fact, of the view that while each side's feelings are understandable, they're deeply flawed at the very core. By the time you're done reading this book, I hope to have you convinced of this point. Many people base their opinion on what they've read and heard on mainstream television, radio and social media. Everyone is a keyboard warrior. In the real-life world what matters most, and what it really boils down to, is that we engage with people and have face-to-face contact.

This book has been long time coming. I feel that modern Australian society deserves answers to frequently asked questions. I believe Australian society is craving answers to these questions. As I will discuss in the next section, it is not that good answers don't exist – because they do. Rather, public debate has been sadly monopolised by those with a political agenda. Instead of hearing a decent and well thought out response to our shared concerns and questions, what we end up hearing are sound bites, slogans and catchphrases, which do nothing to allay our fears.

Another problem that has arisen is that whenever this topic is discussed on the radio or watched on the television, you see either journalists that are out of their depths or a group of high profile Muslim community representatives who appear, simply to want to lay blame of all acts of terrorism on the West and the Zionists. It's as if they don't want to discuss any other possible options or reasons. There appears to be a problematic sense of having no ownership of the problem.

So, overall, we understand that not all of Islam is problematic and we also understand that not all Muslims are terrorists. But since some Muslims certainly are, and they are a very destructive minority within a minority, it's a problem for the leadership of the Muslim community. These leaders must be able to address this with great care and responsibility. However, since their agenda appears to be to talk down the West and the Zionist Jews, their entire effort is concentrated towards that single goal. They must begin to speak out louder when acts of terrorism take place.

As we stand today, any criticism directed at the Islamic community is automatically viewed as Islamophobic or bigoted. Yet, this is only a fraction of the whole problem. Remember, it does take two to tango. So, if we were to turn our focus to the other end of the spectrum, we have a group of journalists and politicians, who are poorly trained and have had very limited exposure into the diverse nature of Islamic communities. There are many interpretations of the Islamic faith. So why do certain individuals believe they are qualified to speak out and prescribe that Islam needs a Reformation?

The format in which this book is structured is quite simple. Through this first section, I am hoping that you have started to know me as a friend; you've come to understand in part what makes me tick and what my motivations are. You have seen a little of the normalcy with which a hard-working Lebanese migrant family raised its Australian-born Muslim daughter. My journey is not the only story of its kind, there are many other Muslims who have led the exact same lifestyle and been raised in the same manner as I was, but they are not all sharing their stories with you. That's something we must change. I truly hold out hope that my book is a welcome start.

My Public Life

I mentioned earlier that I grew up confident and self-reliant. However, one thing that I was not and still am not is an attention seeker. If anything, I tended to avoid too much socialising. This wasn't due to a lack of confidence or shyness as I was not a particularly shy child. It was more a case of humility. I didn't see myself as special. I'm not more or less special than any other person on this planet. I didn't seek attention or try to stand out from the crowd.

I was, and I probably still am, more of a giver than a taker. I've never truly felt comfortable with flattery or praise, no matter how sincere the intent behind it may be. This is as true of my nature today as it was back then. So, you may well ask, what it was that has brought me into the glare of public life? That's a good question! Let me answer it this way, if you had asked me 10 years ago where I saw myself today, I would have told you that I'd be living in my own home, raising children and running a successful business. And I have done exactly that and achieved those aspirations. What I could not have predicted in my wildest dreams would be that I would find my fingers typing on this keyboard, writing this book, the book that you are reading right now. There's no way I could have foreseen what was to come. There have been things that have occurred during the time between my childhood and where I find myself today. These occurrences have forced me to re-assess my views and made me realise that there are some very important problems confronting Australia and they need to be addressed.

Like many other concerned Australians, for years I searched for answers in the rhetoric of the mainstream politicians, but unsurprisingly, I did not find anything useful to assist in answering my questions. One day a quote came to mind and it really resonated with me. That quote was from Mahatma Gandhi and the quote is "Be the change you wish to see in the world".[1] I realised I could be the change that I wanted people to see. It was not that I had interesting ideas, but I realised that having grown up as an Australian Muslim put me in a unique position.

Australian society has seen better days regarding multiculturalism, but we should remember there was a time when people were able to get along with each other. When we look at present political realities, sometimes it's tempting to think that multiculturalism has completely failed us from the beginning.

Yet, how can I forget those times during my childhood when regardless of what background you were from, people banded together behind a common community cause and showed true community spirit. There was no constant threat of terrorism, there was no need for any extra Governmental surveillance or intelligence gathering, there was no need for any crack down on radicals within Muslim communities, and there was certainly a far less likelihood of an Islamic cleric holding a public platform with which they could use publicly to make horrendously stupid comments to the media. The days of my youth really were the good old days.

The spirit of those days needs to be revived. I feel I need to remind people that much of the unrest, we experience today owes itself to the changing patterns of conflict in global politics. Just because Osama Bin Laden had decided to declare war on America and its allies, we did not need to become a part of his war. I never felt that Islam was at war with the West. Yet I remember how rapidly after Bin Laden had arrived on the global scene, so many people in the broader Muslim communities began to sympathise with his declaration of war on American interests.

This bothered me deeply. I recall seeing how easy it was for Muslims during that time to put the blame for failures within their own societies onto America, the Jews and their allies. And their allies included Australia, peaceful old Australia which had nothing to do with the so-called "suffering" of the Muslim ummah at the time. Neither does it today. It never made any sense to me how so many of these people from Muslim backgrounds could feel so much hatred towards the West yet still choose to live in Western countries.

Although as I keep stressing, these were new political attitudes formed in that era. During the 1970s, 1980s and early 1990s, you would not have found too many Arab or Muslim families who held such strong anti-Western views. It is true that a lot of the elders did blame the European colonialism for carving up the Middle East, but there was no political activism associated with this historical event. They casually brought these points up once or twice at the dinner table when discussing history, and that was about as much as politics relating to religion was referred to.

It is also true, that there had always been a degree of scepticism towards Zionism and the State of Israel among Arabs. The Arabs had never truly taken too kindly to the idea of forming a Jewish state situated right in the heart of the traditional Islamic world. After all the wars the Arabs had lost to the Jews, especially the Six Day War in 1967, the animosity towards Israel had become deeply rooted within the Arab psyche.

But again, none of these sentiments were prominent during the era when I was growing up. Throughout my childhood there were no Imams at mosques espousing hatred and inciting violence. During the 1970's, 1980's and early 1990's, there was no rhetoric that was actively encouraging young Arab or Muslim men to go out and target innocent Westerners or Jews seeking revenge for the perceived sufferings of the Islamic "ummah".

Now, this all changed. Hostilities were brought to the fore when Osama Bin Laden's two fatwahs were issued against the United States and its allies. Much of this occurred after the first Gulf War

1990-91 when Iraq invaded Kuwait. The deposed King Al-Sabah requested assistance from the United States. The United States were wanting to station their troops in Saudi Arabia which brought about a great deal of ire and anger from Bin Laden. Bin Laden viewed the installation of US military bases as a sin against Islam and believed this to be a secret plot by the United States to control the politics of oil in the Middle East.

Many Muslims at the time ignored the reality that the US involvement in the Gulf War was largely due to assist in liberating Kuwait, even if there was some self-interest on the part of the US. All countries operate out of self-interest; I'm at a loss to name one country that doesn't operate on this basis. So why would the United States be an exception? As a teenager, I recall pondering these points as the relations between Westerners and Muslims began to worsen and grow wider during the late 1990s.

I distinctly recall that this was the period when Islamist-inspired terrorism started appearing in the news headlines on a regular basis. Prior to Al-Qaeda's terrorism which was inspired by Bin Laden's dictate, the only other major instances of Islamist terrorism were largely limited to Palestinian nationalists and these acts usually only targeted Israeli interests. Most of the world's population did not consider Palestinian terrorism as some sort of a 'clash of civilisations' between Islam and the West. The focus of these attacks was too narrow and weren't directed at the West.

Take for example the 1972 massacre of Israeli athletes by Palestinian gunmen at the Munich Olympics in which 17 innocent people were murdered. Although it was a horrific act of terrorism it was viewed by most of the world as a nationalist struggle. This viewpoint does not justify the violent tactics, the attacks were morally repugnant and horrendous, but people were able to contextualise these attacks as part of Israel's occupation of the West Bank and the Gaza Strip. This attack was too specific in region and intent for it to be misconstrued as an attack against the West.

Now if you look at the Al-Qaeda's terrorism that emerged during the 1990s, this brand of terrorism was directly aimed at the West. It turned out to be a game changer. Bin Laden had essentially urged all Muslims, not just people from one particular ethnic group or nationality, but quite literally anyone and everyone who considered him or herself to be a Muslim to go out and target Americans and their allies and execute them. The message could not have been any clearer.

Bin Laden's attacks on American interests in Africa, the Middle East, Asia and on American soil itself were beginning to make news headlines. Then came September 11, 2001. The world was in shock. Muslim communities worldwide suddenly found themselves needing to explain which side they were on. President Bush called it an attack on Western freedoms and democracy.

Bin Laden's subsequent attacks on American interests in Africa, the Middle East, Asia and on American soil itself were beginning to make news headlines all around the world. Then came September 11, 2001. The world was reeling in shock. Muslim communities worldwide suddenly found themselves needing to explain which side they were on. President Bush called 9/11 an attack on Western freedoms and democracy.

During this time, I felt that the narrative that Bin Laden and his terrorist organisation Al-Qaeda were running was a great deal more complex than the simple rhetoric Bush was espousing. But did it matter anymore? The cat was out of the bag. There were to be consequences. Following 9/11 came the wars in Afghanistan and Iraq. While most Muslims disagreed with Osama Bin Laden and the methods of violence that he used to take his fight to the US, there were also many Muslims who sympathised with Bin Laden's motives.

During the time of Bin Laden's emergence onto the public stage, dormant, anti-colonial and anti-Zionist sentiments which were held by large numbers of Muslims, were translated into physical and violent manifestations of hostility. People seemed to feel they now needed to mobilise politically. Previously, when I was growing up, Muslim elders would have simply made a comment or two that was critical of, say, the United States or Israel and the subject was left at that. After the ever-changing landscape of the 1990s, and especially September 11, 2001, people now found themselves discussing this so-called 'clash of civilisations on a 24/7 basis.

9/11 was front-page news for a long time. Footage was replayed on the news thousands of times over. The average Westerner who watched the footage of the two planes striking the World Trade Centre towers in New York were left wondering, 'Why do Muslims hate us so much? What is it that we have done wrong to deserve this?' Unfortunately, most Westerners have never had the opportunity, to read Bin Laden's two fatwahs. In these two fatwahs, Bin Laden extensively outlines his misguided reasoning for the declaration of war on the United States and its Western allies.

There's no doubt that there was a section of the Muslim community who on the other hand were left wondering why America appeared to be so shocked that after decades of its own legacy of wars, in Korea, Vietnam, Afghanistan and the constant toppling of foreign governments in Iran, Cuba, and other Latin American countries, it had received a little dose of its own medicine. It was an extremely polarising time and many opinions shifted to the extreme ends of the spectrum.

There appeared to be many people who had previously been great supporters of multiculturalism and diversity (like the Anglo-Celtic families I mentioned earlier in the first section) who suddenly found themselves becoming increasingly resistant to immigration, especially Muslim immigration. The fact that leading Australia during these tumultuous times was Prime Minister, John Howard certainly didn't help allay these fears or concerns regarding Islam.

Howard was a staunch conservative and he also had a close relationship with the US President, George Bush. Howard backed and supported all efforts made by the United States to pursue and capture Bin Laden by whatever means necessary. Howard committed Australia to joining the US in its mission to destroy Al-Qaeda and, in the process, crack down hard on Muslim communities living in the US and Australia. To nut out those who were influenced by Bin Laden's way of thinking and who bore a threat to Australia and its allies. Watching these events unfold and seeing the ensuing changes occurring before my very eyes, were almost too much for me to witness. What had happened to the days of sharing food and breaking bread together, shared birthday parties and impromptu street gatherings of my childhood? Why could we not just return to the bliss of the 1970s, 1980s and early 1990s, some may even say, the blissful ignorance? Remorsefully, this was never to be the case or the "norm" again, for 9/11 had shattered that reality or illusion, forever.

There were people who could only understand the viewpoint of the Western world in relation to 9/11 and they truly believed all of Islam was evil. How else can you explain what Al-Qaeda did to us on September 11? There were also those who could only understand this event through an Islamic lens and believed all US foreign policy was imperialistic and Islamophobic. How else do you explain why brown men with beards had to go through extra security checks on domestic and international flights? I feel that due to my background and childhood, I was able to put myself into both sets of shoes and tried to gain an understanding through my lived experiences in both worlds.

My personal experiences had shown me that most people living in the western world were not inherently racist or Islamophobic - not at all. Your average person on the street didn't hold any racial grudges against brown skinned people, regardless of whether they were Indians, Buddhists, Italians or any heritage or religion that you would care to name. I also inherently knew that most Muslims were not evil. Neither were all Muslims indoctrinated into anti-Western democracy or anti-Western freedom thought process. Rather, what I knew to be true of most migrants and their families was that they'd arrived in Australia and had wholeheartedly embraced the country and its culture. These migrant families immigrated to Australia not to change the country but to contribute to its success, to integrate and form a part of Australian society. My own family was a prime example of this societal integration.

So, having these lived experiences to draw upon and having a steadfast belief and knowledge that all Westerners were not racist just as all Muslims are not terrorists, my problem was, how was I able to get this information across to the public? How could I show people, whilst trying to reach a large audience at the same time and impart to them that Islam was not inherently evil and to try and remain calm. It is a tall order, right? I was then caught up tussling with the same question but this time in relation to Islam. How does one truly convince Muslims that the West is not inherently imperialistic? Another tall order, I know. I was not quite sure how to turn my thoughts into positive action, but I knew one thing for certain, and that was, that I had more ideas relating to this issue than the average politician from either of the two major parties seemed to have. This was the beginning of my foray into public life and the driving force behind it.

I felt that as I was an Arabic-speaking Muslim woman, born in Australia, who knew Islam to be a normal and moderate religion as was taught to me by my mum at home. I believed that I could present an alternate view with a different perspective other than the one presented by the mainstream media. Regardless of what the critics of Islam may have espoused and continue to espouse, you will formulate your own opinion over the course of reading this book. But I never forgot that there were literally millions of other Muslims across the globe, who held views and narratives in alignment with my own and where common sense prevailed. Muslim children whose parents were not engaging in any hate speech, were confused as to what was happening and why they were coming under such heavy suspicion. To hold this belief that all Muslims were engaged in teaching hate to their children was essentially to subscribe to the Bin Laden view and narrative of the world.

As I observed earlier on, that upon the release of Bin Laden's fatwahs there were a great many Muslims around the world who found themselves agreeing with Bin Laden and sympathising with his motives. But this is not something I would argue necessarily originates in the authentic teachings of Islam. I felt the mainstream leadership of the Islamic community had failed to get this message across loud and clear. Why? Because half the time they themselves secretly agreed with what Al-Qaeda was fighting for.

I didn't agree with it and I still don't. I don't believe Muslims are some sort of an endangered, oppressed species as so many Islamic clerics make would have you believe. But if the frictions that emerged as a direct result of the rise of Bin Laden's Al-Qaeda and September 11 remained unresolved, then the animosity directed towards Islam and Muslims would continue to be reinforced. In turn that would leave Muslim communities with even more reason to turn anti-Western.

Bin Laden was not an elected representative of any Islamic country on this planet. Even the Islamic country Bin Laden had been born in, Saudi Arabia, had stripped him of his citizenship. He became a fugitive, a political dissident running from one country to the next, Sudan, Afghanistan and finally to Pakistan where he was eventually located and executed by the US military in 2011.

During the time, I witnessed first-hand how polarised the world had become. I saw how this widespread polarisation had taken place since the rise of Al-Qaeda and the countless, suicide bombing attacks that followed. Due to these attacks and the constantly changing political realities, alarmingly Muslims found themselves torn between the moderates and extremists.

There came a point where I thought to myself, 'enough is enough'. I could no longer sit back and allow this to happen. I decided I had to engage in positive action. I purposefully began to engage even further with my local community through attending local RSL clubs, local churches as well as football clubs, to try and start conversations of meaning with my fellow school and sports parents. I attempted to get to know more of my community on that old, first name basis. It was powerful and necessary action for me to take. It expanded my understanding of my community and it felt good that the local community were comfortable meeting and engaging with someone like me. After all, I was an average, normal, moderate, mainstream Australian Muslim woman who was living a happy and productive life, just like so many other mainstream Australians.

Sometimes, the simple act of having a conversation with someone may lead to helping that person diffuse their fears, concerns and possible anxieties. During these conversations, I wasn't simply on a mission to make Westerners love Islam or Muslims, far from it. The truth was that over the years, I had encountered and taken mental note of many flaws within the Muslim communities that I felt needed to be addressed. Please don't for a moment fall prey to the assumption I believe the Muslim community is above criticism!

During the height of this so-called 'clash of civilisations', many of the migrants granted entry to Australia were not the ideal types of migrants. A large proportion of these migrants were dependant on our welfare system and they often seemed to be able to find shortcuts around Australia's legal and political systems. Previously, when One Nation leader Pauline Hanson first emerged into the limelight of Australian politics, her key focus was on tackling Asian immigration and Indigenous welfare dependency that was occurring during this time.

Two decades later, One Nation's and Pauline Hanson's primary focuses are addressing and solving the issues Australia is facing, such as Muslim immigration, problems with radicalisation, and the failure of migrants to properly integrate. Successful integration means to be successfully functioning within Australian society.

There are a great many Australians who hold the same views as One Nation; I am one of those people. I don't believe for a moment the corruption that was and is still rampant within Islamic communities could be ignored. Neither do I believe that any Muslim who believes Bin Laden's rhetoric against the West should be allowed to remain in Australia. These strong convictions pushed me in the direction of being the change that I so dearly wished to see in the world.

The next question I faced when I made the decision to try and enact this change was, how and on what platform would I best be able to have my thoughts heard and taken seriously. It was important not be just seen within Australia but globally too, as this was and is most certainly a global problem.

I decided that my best course of action would be to utilise social media as so many people such as celebrities and public figures do, this enables them to have their messages read, listened to and discussed. I started by writing posts on social media to try to engage people and for them to gain an understanding of the issues that are facing both "sides". I wanted to start discussions that may not otherwise have been started. In today's era of technology, people can connect with so many others online from the comfort of their smartphones, so I used that to my advantage. I tried to connect with people and enable a discourse relating to these issues to start, and hopefully gain momentum. My posts did begin to gain traction. I had many people reach out to me and to thank me for having the courage to step forward and to present my opinions so openly and with no bias for or against Muslim Australians and non-Muslim Australians. I had people from all over the globe sending me messages of support, people who followed a religion, not just Muslims but also Christians and Catholics, people who were secular and people who were just scared and unsure, the messages came everywhere from Australia to Spain and many countries in between.

From the messages and the amount of subscribers my posts received, I was sure that the people who were reading my posts were able to recognise within me, the ability to explain the West to Muslims and also have the same ability to explain and make sense of Islam to Westerners, in a manner that I believe hasn't been seen to date. The genuine empathy that I shared with them over their concerns resonated with the people who were reading my posts, and each day my subscriber base grew. A lot of prominent voices who were already involved in the social activist space also reached out to me. A few years ago, I found myself invited to a Libertarian conference in my hometown of Sydney. That event led me to a very interesting turning point in what had morphed into my "public life".

At the Libertarian conference I met the man who took on Liberal Prime Minister John Howard in the hotly contested federal election of 2014. That's right, I met former Labor leader Mark Latham at the conference, and little did I know the profound affect that Mark would have on the direction that my 'public figure' life would take. Mark showed an appreciation of my stance on the issues that I have been publicly discussing and the appreciation was mutual. I discussed with Mark my admiration for him and I respected the fact he had he never left the Labor Party, but rather the Labor Party had left him. Mark, as I quickly discovered, was a man of conviction. We held many of the same convictions and this sat comfortably with me. Mark encouraged me to remain steadfast in my convictions and my passion to pursue a public life and to continue onwards and make the difference I wanted to see. It was a fortuitous meeting and Mark has since become my mentor much to my surprise and appreciation.

As I began to venture out and meet a multitude of people to discuss and share my ideas with, I soon started encountering many others who were highly active on the social media scene. Admittedly some of these encounters were more colourful than others but it was through these that I was able to glean a better understanding and gain insightful revelations. One of these revelations was that there is certainly no shortage of people who claim that they would like to see more moderate Muslims step forward, to call out and condemn the extremists living within their communities. This call for action was prevalent on a variety of social media platforms, blogs, opinion pieces, newspapers and in mainstream media. There was a continuous calling out from commentators for a public condemnation to be issued by the leaders of the Islamic communities for the atrocities committed.

People repeatedly comment to me that they personally do not have a problem with religion, race or ethnicity but rather, the problem appears to be the lack of integration into Western society. The thing that strikes me as odd about this statement is that in theory it sounds feasible to expect that migrants arriving in a new country should be able to integrate into the culture of the country they have voluntarily chosen to travel to and to call their new home. But this seamless integration is just not occurring for a myriad of reasons. I explore the reasons why this integration is not working successfully at length in the last chapter of the book.

The problem facing us presently appears to be that none of these promoters of integration and assimilation can succinctly define what is meant when they use these terms. What is the definition of true integration and what does assimilation look like in real life? Most importantly, how do we arrive at that place? This too is a topic that I discuss in greater detail in a chapter further into the book. The problem as I see it is, if you are placing expectations on migrants entering Australia, but you are unable to articulate and explain these notions of integration and assimilation, how can the migrants fulfil these expectations? It's as if you are expecting people to behave in a certain manner, which you are unable to explain yourself. My view on integration and assimilation into Australian society comes from having respect for democracy, respect for our rule of law, respect for the fundamental equality of the two genders, respect for people's sexual orientation, respect for people's right to choose to live their lives the way they see fit as long as they are not harming anybody else or breaking any laws.

Many people upon hearing the terms integration and assimilation have a pre-conceived image in their mind of someone behaving and sounding like the true-blue Aussie stereotype. As I discuss in the last section of this book, having an Aussie accent or dressing like an Aussie doesn't automatically mean that you are loyal to Australia. If you were to visit Lakemba then you would encounter many anti-Western types but you will find that they appear and sound perfectly Australian. You would be none the wiser to their anti-West sentiments.

So, my own personal definition of integration and assimilation, when applied to our society is the act of wholeheartedly accepting the countries' core values as I mentioned and outlined above. It is this *respect* for a whole range of social norms and customs that is often absent in undemocratic societies this is how I would describe true integration and assimilation. By this very definition, I am about as integrated an Australian Muslim as you will ever find.

This in turn leads to my next crucial point: taking issue with those who demand integration and assimilation but when they do see it in action, they find fault with it. Take someone such as myself, who respects democracy, the Australian rule of law, gender equality, freedom of sexual choice, I embody the Australian values, yet I am still attacked by those who call for assimilation. They find fault with me and tell me and other moderates that we don't know our own religion, or that we are wolves in sheep's clothing and accuse us of being Muslim apologists. From where I sit, you are damned if you do assimilate into Australian culture and damned if you don't.

I am not easily boxed into one category. I hold many different views over a wide range of subjects. This sometimes confuses and irritates people. I would like to note that this book is not aimed at any particular demographic, rather I wrote it for people who have an open mind and who have the courage to have their biases challenged, left wing biases, right wing biases and whatever other biases that may lay between them.

I am not suggesting that people hold these biases on a conscious level with a maliciously planned agenda but rather they stem from an unconscious level of bias, stemming from the unknown. I think they may also hold these biases because they are not sure exactly what it is that they seek in the ideal migrant.

To my way of thinking a migrant does not have to totally forget or stop practicing the traditions from their culture of origin or from their upbringing. Not only is that an impossible ask on a human level but it is totally unnecessary. When German migrants in Australia continue to celebrate Oktoberfest or the Irish celebrate St Patrick's Day, they are not viewed with suspicion and asked to give up their cultural traditions. In fact, many non-Irish and non-German citizens partake in these annual festivities with mighty gusto.

Tradition and cultural practices don't have to be forgotten nor left behind, if they are not directly opposed to Australian values. For example, if in a family culture the daughter is expected to to marry a man, whom her family has already chosen as her husband, rather than the choice being her own, Australians expect that tradition to be thrown into the bin the minute you land on Australian soil. This not only applies to Muslim culture but any cultural group within Australia where their cultural practices do not co-exist with Australian values or laws. This is the type of scenario that many advocates of migrant integration don't really discuss or explain in detail via a public platform that reaches mainstream Australia. This in turn can create problems for the migrants arriving in Australia and simultaneously fuels fear in the minds of the Australian public with regard to migrants and their cultures, including their cultural practices.

As a result, many in the general population will view the arriving immigrants with suspicion and distrust due to a lack of knowledge and understanding of these cultural differences. This is due, in part, to the deafening silence surrounding these points of difference from all levels of government, as well as silence from migration integration advocates and specialists. There appears to be a lack of public discourse surrounding these cultural differences. Honest and frank discussions should be initiated by the local, state and federal government as well as the myriad of migration advocates who have a thorough understanding of the issues facing immigrants.

The flow on effect of holding pre-existing misconceptions and assumptions appears to be that many people upon meeting or encountering a Muslim out in public who may be wearing their traditional and cultural clothing such as an Imam may don, is that they either have a very conscious or sub-conscious distrust of these individuals. Regardless of whether the individual they are observing is a law abiding, decent Muslim who contributes to Australian society by working and paying taxes, has integrated into Australian society, whose loyalty and love of Australia is unshakeable, and who is an asset to this country, there still seems to be this underlying current of distrust. I have encountered people who, upon meeting such a Muslim, hold an inherent belief there is still something afoot and you can never truly trust an "integrated" Muslim. They believe that although this person may appear decent, it's only because they are not a true Muslim or that they are just biding time until a so called caliphate is called and all Muslims will turn on 'infidels' and will attempt to kill them all. Nothing could be further from the truth, a fundamental reason and part of the intent behind writing this book is to challenge such assumptions and misconceptions.

It is entirely possible to be Muslim and retain your religion and the acceptable cultural practices that come with being Muslim, as well as be Australian who is loyal and committed to the success of this country and its people. Being Muslim and a patriotic Australian are not mutually exclusive. The calibre and commitment of Muslims who consider themselves to be Australian first and foremost is widespread throughout Australian communities. I will re-iterate again that most Muslims are good people whose loyalties lay with Australia.

Sadly, there are many migrants entering Australia who do not abide to the Australian laws and cultural expectations. One example of this would be the recent crime waves involving migrants, particularly in our state of Victoria at the time of writing this book. But there are also many migrants arriving in Australia who are working hard to assimilate and make the most of the opportunities they have been afforded. Although, we rarely hear about these successful integration stories because they don't make attention-grabbing news articles. Each person arriving in Australia, from various countries, arrives with their own cultural identities, they experience personal and individual difficulties along with a shared set of difficulties common among migrants. Muslims are no exception.

I have shared some of my experiences in this book, knowing that there are many other Muslims like me, who may find it difficult to speak out due to a lack of public platform. Some don't want to draw attention to themselves. Others are busy tending to their daily lives and are already part of that successfully woven tapestry of Australian community which is often neglected by extremists who blanket their dislike of all Muslims and crying out, 'integration will never work'. Being a Muslim as well as being a proud, law abiding, Australia loving, citizen is not mutually exclusive. Rather they can and do co-exist harmoniously. I personally know so many others who think just like me. They love Islam in its mainstream normative form (as described throughout various sections of this book) and at the same time, love Australia.

Unfortunately, there are many Muslims who would like to contribute to this discussion but don't feel confident in speaking out or are too shy to voice their opinions publicly. We need to encourage and support Muslims who would like to become active on social media, or to start a blog or a YouTube channel, to do just that and to become part of this important discussion. One of the myriads of reasons I felt compelled to write this book is to inspire people to speak out, to voice their opinions and thoughts with the wider community. I would like others within the Muslim community to join me in this discussion, I want to be the start of a cavalcade of voices to join me and contribute to the wider debate on Islam, Muslims and life in the West.

As you will note as you read this book, I devote a substantial portion to discussing successful integration versus the extremist elements within the Muslim community. These elements are an integral ingredient in the ongoing distrust and confusion by the West, which surround the true nature of Islam and Muslims. But it is not just the extremist elements that I turn my attention to, there are many non-Muslim as well as Muslim critics of Islam who also come under scrutiny and are not exempt from criticism. We have a long way to go regarding making integrated Muslims feel welcome in right wing circles. The next time you meet a person who may be a proud Conservative or Libertarian or simply proud to be Australian, please do not make hasty assumptions about these people because they also happen to identify as Muslim.

As a society, we appear very quick to judge and condemn a person based on their religion, beliefs or opinions. I think we need to ease the pressure a little, cut some slack, treat each person respectfully as an individual first and foremost. Rather than searching for contradictions in what is being said, or trying to make the individual appear stupid in front of others, just so that an agenda can be furthered, we should be engaging our listening, critical thinking skills and evaluate what is being discussed before casting our judgement upon an individual. This is an issue that all those who describe themselves as right of centre can work on improving.

It was after much deliberation over these matters I decided I would take my public life beyond mere social media. That is the reason why I decided to join Pauline Hanson's One Nation Party. The fact that I joined One Nation may surprise you, but without a doubt, Pauline Hanson is among the most widely misunderstood and arguably the least appreciated of all Australian politicians. For those of us who know her personally, Pauline is a hardworking, ordinary Australian mother, not dissimilar to me. Pauline is neither a racist nor an Islamophobe. She loves Australia and its people, regardless of how long ago our ancestors arrived in Australia whether it be 40,000 years, 200 years or merely 50 years ago. The colour-blind attitude that Pauline holds resonated well with me and was very similar to the attitude in my childhood household where were raised to respect diversity and culture and not to judge people based upon religion, heritage or country of birth.

Pauline is a woman with strong convictions; convictions which she will stand by and defend to her own personal detriment if need be. Her media appearances are not scripted, and Pauline speaks directly from the heart. In many ways Pauline reminds me of myself and I share the same view as Pauline that the two major political parties that govern Australia have lost their way. The two major parties have been reduced to empty rhetoric, broken promises and repetitive slogans which have denigrated into a 'he said, she said' style of discourse. These realisations contributed towards my decision to meet with Pauline Hanson and join One Nation, to ensure that we could, together, keep our country, its culture and its way of life intact. At the time of my joining One Nation in 2019 I believed One Nation members who were having concerns about my membership and my candidate nomination within the Hornsby electorate in NSW, would come to realise that as an Australian Muslim there would be a great deal that I could contribute to One Nation. And I also vehemently believe there are more Muslims such as myself who must step forward and speak their truth. To voice out loud and proud, 'we love Australia and our loyalties are with Australia and its best interests and want to preserve and protect the Australian way of life'. I hoped this would give rise to the critics and sceptics of Islam changing their stance a little. Plus, I hoped it would open the possibility of a constructive and respectful dialogue pertaining to their fears and concerns.

Why did I feel confident about this? Because I have a good grasp and understanding of the Australian cultural psyche and the flexibility of Australians to amend their views and opinions when presented with compelling reasoning. There are many areas within the world whereby rivalries over race, religion, ethnicity can create tensions, violence and destruction. Take for example the mutual dislike and distrust between many countries such as Indian and Pakistan, Greece and Macedonia, Serbia and Croatia, or the continual unrest between Israel and Palestine.

In Australia, we have no such equivalent conflict. The extent to which you might find Australia poking others in the eye is pretty much limited to sports, for the most part. Yes, we like to give it to the Poms during the Ashes, and to the Kiwis when we face the All Blacks, but we love 'em, and we know they love us. Men and women will go and share a drink and a meal together afterwards and whatever good-natured rivalry there may be, it's all in fun and makes for much frivolity, laughter and elbow poking.

Australians are not naturally prone to blind hatred and when upset it is usually in response to a perceived wrong or perceived threat to the Australian way of life. So, all the anxiety and confusion that people hold surrounding Islam and Muslims are for understandable reasons as well as in part, based on irrational fears and misnomers. With this in mind, I realised in advance that within the One Nation membership there would those who were distrustful, sceptical and confused as to why I would join One Nation.

This distrustfulness and scepticism were something that I had expected. I looked forward to dispelling that distrust and scepticism. I innately understood that if you want people to know that not all Muslims are inherently evil terrorists and nor are all interpretations of Islam intrinsically extreme, then the last thing I should be attempting is to try and hammer my points down people's throats the way many Islamic community leaders tend to do on mainstream media. This approach has never been constructive or successful. I believe the best way to illustrate this is to be the change that you want to see, live pro-actively and stand as living proof and testament to this.

I was the embodiment of this approach. To what extent has this worked? This question is an intriguing one and there is no simple answer. On the one hand, I had countless people come and greet me, welcome me onboard. Some people were genuinely surprised to meet a moderate Muslim woman who was outspoken in her views and has a fierce love and loyalty to Australia and all that it stands for. Through this exposure I was afforded to the opportunity to express my views and to publicly remind people that there are so many other Muslims who hold similar views and convictions such as myself. When I see a spade, I call the spade. I encourage other Muslims to do the same and hope to create and encourage further dialogue. My outlook and my views on multi-culturalism, Muslims and the role of Islam resonated well with many of the One Nation members, Pauline and her hard-working loyal staff.

This was not the case with all One Nation members and Pauline lost many members and supporters for endorsing a Muslim for a One Nation candidacy. I hold no ill will towards these One Nation members or supporters and welcome the opportunity to illustrate the benefits of having me on board. I had been expecting a fall-out to some degree over my candidacy. As I have mentioned, the anxieties and worries that people hold surrounding Muslims and Islam are quite understandable and these concerns are of varying magnitude, but I do not believe these concerns come from a place of malice but rather from misunderstanding or through misinformation.

Many people I've met who hold these types of views and opinions are very open to discussion and engaging in constructive discussion. When presented with an alternate view of Islam and Muslims, they can raise their concerns and have their questions, worries and fears allayed. Many people then hold a different perception of Muslims compared to the view they previously held.

On the other hand, many detractors of Islam are not open to taking part in a dialogue or addressing the concerns they hold surrounding Muslims and Islam. They have an extreme, blanket opinion that anything to do with Islam is evil and all Muslims are untrustworthy, liars and terrorists. In their mind you cannot be Australian and Muslim, they believe that both are mutually exclusive.

I think we can safely say that we are in agreeance, Australia has an issue with Islam and the ensuing problems associated with Muslim immigration. One barrier faced is that the Muslim detractors have very loud voices which are heard on many platforms, but they do not have any positive input on how to rectify the problem. The irony is the detractors are themselves part of the overall problem and in no way, shape or form do they contribute towards a workable, constructive solution. They don't want to be part of that solution. Furthermore, in their mind, there is no solution rather than to remove all Muslims from Australia.

The reality of this solution is there are over half a million Muslims within Australia; some have currently arrived through immigration and many others who are second or third generation Australians who were born in this country. How can you deport these Muslims? Where would you deport them to? This so-called solution has no merit, it doesn't make sense and isn't a practical answer to any issue that surrounds Australia and Islam. Going forward, we can toughen our immigration policies, but the question would then follow 'what do we do with the Muslim population already living in Australia?'.

I find the proposition of deporting all Muslims from Australia an incredibly preposterous idea. The majority of Muslims in Australia are Australian born, law abiding patriotic Australian citizens. According to the 2016 Australian Census, "the combined number of people who self-identified as Muslim in Australia, from all forms of Islam, constituted 604,200 people, or 2.6% of the total Australian population" and also concluded "that more than half are non-practicing"[3] cultural Muslims stemming from all the varying denominations and sects of Islam present in Australia".

To begin with, there's an undesirable element across all ethnicities, religions and communities, and this problematic behaviour must be weeded out regardless of religious denomination. Australia and its citizens must illuminate the path, come together to address this and to work towards a place of harmony and co-existence. Rather than to eliminate our differences we need to celebrate them as these differences form part of the beautiful woven tapestry that is Australian society. This is a tapestry that has been woven over the centuries by all whom have arrived on Australia's shores.

When we broach the subject of radicalisation, I would like to see that that Muslim Community Leaders have failed to inspire loyalty and respect for Australia among the wider Muslim community. There is a void; a void of role-models for young Muslims to look up to and emulate. What is needed to fill this void? We need more people like me to speak out and to keep contradicting the typical Muslim stereotype, we need a greater focus on the integrated Muslim population that already exists within Australia and look toward them to see what they are doing to make this integration successful. This would serve to show non-Muslim Australians that there are many good, committed, loyal, proud to be Australian Muslims living within a broad range of communities and would also highlight to Muslim Australians that this is how co-existence, respect and harmonious communities look like, not the depiction portrayed to them by radical Imams.

Many Muslims do not need these role models; their own actions and integration into Australia are already in place.

What I do find interesting is the reaction within the Muslim community when I announced my candidacy for One Nation. I had many Muslims contact me to express the fact they were sick and tired of the focus and publicity on Muslims who are not integrating and doing wrong by Australia. They observed that this tends to tar all Muslims with the same brush. There are so many Muslims who are Australian who live, work, practice their religion and have achieved seamless integration that it's often overlooked in favour of reporting on the negative side of Muslim integration.

On the flip side of this though, I have been approached by Muslims who cannot understand how I identify as a Muslim yet could join and run as a candidate for One Nation. To their way of thinking, Pauline Hanson was the epitome of old school 'White Australia Policy' style racism from yesteryear. I know this is not the truth, but those Muslims upset at my decision to join One Nation still had this old stereotype in their minds. There was no way I could convince them otherwise. They are dogmatic in their stance and run on emotion and not logic. Ironically, these Muslims are branches of the same tree as those who quit One Nation when I came on board. The people who cannot be reasoned with whether they be Muslim or non-Muslim need not be worried about. They are outnumbered by the sensible majority.

Upon meeting Mark Latham, I have come to realise there is so much one can do to shape public thinking and influence policy outcomes without ever having to join either of the major two political parties which dominate our political landscape. Australian culture is inherently geared towards scepticism when it is in relation towards anyone in authority. We do not like being spoken down to or taken as fools and therefore you will see CEOs of big companies, politicians, captains of sporting teams, all going out of their way to act as 'first among equals'. Australians like to be treated as equals and to be treated in the same manner as you would a mate.

Suffice to say, Mark does not fall short of living up to this Aussie standard. Mark treats all people as equal and he has been an incredible tower of support for me. He's my mentor whilst treating me with respect, equality and mateship. If more Australians had a greater understanding of Mark, his policies and motivations there would be less distrust and scepticism towards One Nation — and possibly politicians in general.

It is certainly true that some people enter politics for the wrong reasons. Some enjoy the perks that come with being a politician as well as their ego being fed along with their lust for power. Fortunately, though there are individuals who are driven by principles and the best interests of Australia who enter politics and it is these individuals who are the strength and backbone of Australian politics.

Mark has a great deal of experience and knowledge. He's a veteran when it comes to Australian politics. He is now treading down a new path, away from the two-party political system, Mark can see what ails Australia and holds the same views as your every day, average Australian. Mark wants to make a difference in the Australian people's lives and personifies Mahatma Gandhi's infamous quote, "You must be the change you want to see in the world."

Not only does Mark want to be that change and make that difference and he feels that his role as an Upper House MP in the New South Wales Legislative Council would best enable him to make that difference. When Mark and I first met at a Libertarian conference some years ago, I was full of energy and ideas and Mark instantly recognised that about me. But what I lacked was the necessary political experience needed to survive on the path to making a difference in Australian politics and Australian's lives.

I do not present myself as having learnt the ropes at this stage, but with the clarity of hindsight I am confident in the knowledge that I am a great deal more enlightened today then I was when I first forayed into the political world. It is not easy to be in the glare of the public eye. It's imperative you find a healthy balance between achieving your goals and balancing public life. It is a balance to address and push for issues which are important to you whilst fending off those who will try to belittle you, refuse to give you credit where credit is due, or are all too eager to point out your failings or to discredit you at any opportunity.

But life is not fair, equal or kind in the political world or in the real world. Politics is a rough and tumble game, which is neither fair nor equal and whoever first made the statement that "a political life isn't meant for everyone" was a wise person and hit the nail on the head. That said, I am a pretty stoic person and it is virtually impossible to offend me. In the short time that I have been in public life, I have met a wide range of people on my journey thus far who have sat at varying places along the continuum. I'm pretty sure it's the same with any other lifestyle or career choice. Every pathway comes with its fair share of challenges and I am here, determined, ready, able and willing to face these challenges.

At this point you should now have a better understanding of my motivations and reasons for attaining a presence on social media, and later joining One Nation. What you will read in this book is only the beginning. There is still much to be achieved in the quest for a harmonious, equitable, safe world in which to raise our children. It is my hope that as you read through the chapters in this book, you will be presented with a view of Islam that is not often seen by the West.

My sincerest wish in putting pen to paper and writing this book is to challenge much of what you thought you knew about the Islamic religion and to dispel commonly held myths pertaining to Islam and Muslims. Finally, I hope to inspire many more Muslims to step forward and speak out. At the same time, it will hopefully inspire many more Australians to seek a more nuanced view about Islam.

2

ISLAM
A BASIC OVERVIEW

Who would disagree that since the horrific events of September 11, 2001, Islam has become the most discussed religion in the Western world? In a way, it's sad this even has to be the starting point for this section. An understandable anxiousness seems pervasive and appears to be widespread. This is a true reflection of how many people feel towards Islam.

It remains so widespread for two main reasons. One, terrorist acts in the name of Islam continue to occur on far too regular a basis. And two, no one has yet made a serious effort to call a spade 'a spade' and get to the root of the problem due to political correctness.

Yes, there are academics that write about these issues. But let's be honest, they write for a highly academic audience and often overcomplicate things, which makes it hard for people to follow what they're trying to get at. There are committed journalists who write about this topic too, but let us face it, there is only so much that can be summed up in a typical thousand-word article. So, the result is, they oversimplify the issues in ways that often allow for people's anxieties to be further reinforced, as opposed to being brought to a calm.

While I am definitely not an expert on this topic and won't even pretend to be one, what I can say with great confidence is that often the best way to understand a culture is by walking in the shoes of those who follow it and by seeing the world as they see it.

I bring you that experience about Islam and Muslims in this section. This is something many of those so-called experts are unable to provide. This section will neither overcomplicate the subject like academics nor oversimplify it like the journalists. I will do my best to address the issues that you have always wanted to see addressed without political correctness.

At the end of the day, we don't see terrorism being committed in the name of any other religion. So, it is fair to then pose the question, why is this occurring. This cannot be answered without first understanding a little bit about the religion itself. So, let's get started.

What is Islam?

Islam is a religion. It comes with its own set of beliefs, a whole bunch of stuff that its followers accept as 'fact'. It comes with its own set of values made up of a whole stack of DOs and DON'Ts that followers are expected to live by. The same is true of any other religion. Islam sees itself as a continuation of the tradition of the Biblical Prophet Abraham, who both Jews and Christians also believe in. Just as Christianity saw itself as a fulfilment of Judaism, Islam sees itself as a fulfilment of both Judaism and Christianity. This makes it difficult to properly get one's head around Islam without having a basic insight into these earlier two religions that came before it.

Islam's basic assumption is that there is only one God, as opposed to multiple gods or goddesses. It assumes this God is just and kind, that he created the universe and all life within it to be worshipped.[2] Islam holds that angels were the original creation of God, they did as they were told to and worshipped him day and night without fail. It holds that God wanted to test to see if he were to make a creature that had conscious free will, i.e. the ability to think independently, would that creature still choose to love and worship God, unlike the angels who hadn't, until that point in time, disobeyed him. God then created Adam, the first male human, later his wife Eve, the first female human. God was pleased with Adam's creation and he asked the angels to bow before him.

All of them did so, except one. He became the fallen angel, or Satan. He is known to Christians as Lucifer and to Muslims as Iblees. The fallen angel was so jealous of Adam he swore to create havoc among all of God's creation and to mislead them from worshipping him. If God had so chosen, he could have put Iblees in his place and destroyed him right there and then. But instead, God accepted his challenge with great confidence that the righteous among his creation would never side with Iblees over him anyway. It didn't take long before Iblees had his first crack at misleading humanity. Adam and his wife Eve were told to live and enjoy life in a special place called the Garden of Eden. Their only major instruction was to avoid eating the fruit of a certain tree.

Satan convinced Eve to eat this forbidden fruit by whispering into her ear. She not only fell for it, but also went and convinced Adam to do the same. God became angry at Adam and Eve being misled by Iblees and sent them to live on earth as punishment. This sets the stage for the battle between God and Satan - or good and evil - that would go on to defining the course of the human condition. From this moment on, God's objective would be to reveal a set of guidelines for the descendants of Adam and Eve (i.e. us humans) to live by, Satan's objective on the other hand would be to turn us away from doing God's will.

Islam believes that humans are born pure and free from sin. Each newborn child has an in-built sense of differentiating between right and wrong. This is called *fitrah* in Arabic. Over time, people become corrupted by their environment, culture, upbringing or life experiences. Islam says that in order to lead us to the righteous path in this battle between good and evil, God has sent countless noble individuals to deliver his message to humanity. These are called prophets.

Islam follows in the tradition of Judaism and Christianity and accepts as valid all the prophets mentioned in the Old and New Testaments. Islam accepts the story that the one true God is that deity who spoke to Moses on Mount Sinai and revealed the Ten Commandments. It also believes it was the same God who sent Jesus as the Messiah and prophet to humanity. Because Islam sees itself a continuation of Jewish tradition, it is important to spend a bit of time trying to get our heads around how Judaism started.

Judaism as a religion began more than 3,000 years ago, although it hasn't always been known by the label 'Judaism'. Its story began in a region which on today's world map would be somewhere around southern Iraq. The land was known as Ur. This was a timeframe when most people in the Middle East used to worship multiple gods and goddesses. It is against this backdrop that the story of Abraham begins.

He was a pious man, and a prophet, who detested the idea of worshipping multiple gods. He believed there could only be one God who was master of the whole universe. For a long time, Abraham struggled to have a son through his wife Sarah. At a very old age, he had a son through his Egyptian maid Hagar. They named him Ishmael. Eventually he ended up having a second son through his wife Sarah. They named him Isaac.

Abraham left Hagar and Ishmael in the wilderness, took his wife Sarah and their son Isaac and migrated westwards as God commanded him to. God promised to make great nations after both of Abraham's sons. Isaac had a son himself by the name of Jacob who then became a father of twelve sons himself. It is through these twelve sons of Jacob that we get the twelve tribes of Israel. One of those sons was *Judah* and the land of Israel or Palestine, was traditionally named *Judea* after this son. It is through this that we get the words *Jew* or *Jewish*.

Meanwhile Ishmael goes on to have twelve sons himself, from whom, we get the tribes of Arabia. You would have often heard Jews and Arabs referred to as 'cousins' or related ethnic groups. Now you know why; it's because Jews come from Isaac while Arabs come from Ishmael. Isaac's son Jacob's other name was *Israel*, which is why the Jews are often referred to as the *Beni Israel* in both Hebrew and Arabic, which means 'Children of Israel'.

Islam accepts that God sent many prophets to the Children of Israel. All the prophetic stories within Judaism are held as valid by Islam. The Jewish people were enslaved in Egypt then rescued by the Prophet Moses. God promised them the land of Israel. They set up a Jewish Kingdom there and experienced prosperity. King Solomon built a beautiful temple.

They were then invaded multiple times and held in captivity by the Assyrians, Babylonians, Greeks and Romans. Constant invasions and destruction lead the Jews to develop a belief in a Messiah, a special figurehead who would come and rescue them from constant foreign invasions, occupation, exile and enslavement.

Jesus came along 2,000 years ago and claimed to be that Jewish Messiah — at a time when Jews were ruled by the Romans. Jesus was accused of being a troublemaker and sentenced to death by crucifixion. Those who obeyed Jesus at first became another Messianic sect of Judaism. But most Jews did not accept Jesus as their promised Messiah for reasons that go beyond the scope of this book.

This is the point at which Judaism and Christianity deviate courses as two separate religions. Jewish struggles for independence from Rome continued regardless. Rome came down hard and crushed Jewish revolts and, in the process, ended up destroying the Jewish Temple in Jerusalem. It is important to note this is the second time the Jewish Temple is destroyed. The first was by the Babylonians a few centuries earlier.

The Romans kicked the Jews out of Jerusalem beginning what has come to be known as the Jewish *diaspora*. That is, a condition in which the Jews are separated from their ancestral and religious homeland, left to be scattered around the world. Jewish Rabbis develop the two commentaries on Jewish religion. These are called the two Talmuds. Jews have long yearned to return to their homeland for the remaining 2,000 years of this diaspora.

Meanwhile Jesus and his disciples saw themselves as Jews, but due to their practices that differed from mainstream Jews in their day, this Jewish sect basically developed into a religion of its own and became Christianity. Christians to date insist that Jesus fulfilled the Jewish prophecy by dying on the cross while Jews to date reject this view and are waiting for what they consider to be the 'real' Messiah to come. Christianity was at first severely persecuted by the Roman Empire for its initial three centuries, until the Romans somewhat ironically ended up embracing the very religion, they had gone out of their way to persecute. The year 381 marks the official adoption of Christianity as Rome's state religion.

Islam's founder, the Prophet Muhammad, believed he was receiving revelations from the same God who spoke to the Jewish Prophet Moses on Mount Sinai and to Jesus Christ in the Galilee. Islam does not believe Judaism and Christianity to be 'false' religions; in fact, it believes they were both divine revelations that are now obsolete because Islam has taken over as the final testament.

In terms of both theology and the day-to-day practices, Islam is like

Orthodox Judaism. In that, both are strict rules-based religions with their own dietary laws about what adherents can and can't eat, daily prayers with specific items of worship facing specific directions.

Note that Jews are required to pray three times a day facing Jerusalem while Muslims are required to pray five times a day facing Mecca. There are strict laws regarding marriage, birth, inheritance, death, divorce, property, contract and various civil wrongs. Christianity by contrast lacks this legalistic dimension that features so prominently in both Judaism and Islam.

Islam is heavily focussed on the hereafter, which is life beyond death. Islam stresses that the life of this world is only a 'test' by God Almighty, Allah, to see if we are able to distinguish between good and evil, and live by his instructions. Unlike in Christianity where if one believes in Jesus as their lord and saviour, their sins are forgiven with paradise guaranteed, Islam offers no such promises. It makes you work for your salvation by living according to the rites, rituals and rules of Islam.

In the most basic sense, Islam has five pillars each Muslim must do his or her level best to try and live by.[3] These are:

1) *Shahada* (Testimony): That is to testify in the belief that there is no God but Allah and Muhammad is his last and final Prophet.

2) *Salah* (Worship): That is to perform the daily prayers five times facing Mecca. Each of the five prayers has a name, these are: *Fajr* (morning prayer), *Zuhr* (midday prayer), *Asr* (late afternoon prayer), *Maghrib* (sunset prayer) and *Isha* (evening prayer).

3) *Zakat* (Charity): That is to give a minimum of 2.5% of your annual savings away to the poor and needy.

4) *Sawm* (Fasting): That is to fast in the month of *Ramadan*,

which means no eating or drinking from sunrise until sunset.

5) *Hajj* (Pilgrimage): That is to visit the city of Mecca and perform the prescribed rituals at the black cube-shaped building called the *Kaba*.

This is Islam summed up in a nutshell. The next section deals with some of its basic history.

When and how did Islam start?

Islam views itself, not as a new religion so to speak, but rather as a continuation of the earlier traditions of Judaism and Christianity. In this sense, Muslims believe Islam began with Adam and Eve. They believe the Jewish prophets mentioned in the Old Testament from Noah, Abraham, Isaac, Jacob, Moses, David, Solomon, through to Elijah as 'Muslims'. From the New Testament, John the Baptist and Jesus are also part of the mix as 'Muslim' prophets. So, Muhammad is seen not as the founder of a new movement, but rather as the last and final prophet in a long series of prophets that began with Adam himself, the first human created by God as discussed in the previous section.

At the time of Muhammad's birth in 570, Arabia was religiously divided.[4] There were communities of Jews who lived around Medina, pagan Arabs who lived around Mecca, and dispersed across both cities were pockets of various Christian communities, as well as followers of other forms of religious practices such as sun and moon worshipping.

As discussed in the previous section, the Jews descend from Abraham through his son Isaac, the Arabs descend from Abraham through his son Ishmael. After Abraham takes his wife Sarah and their son Isaac westwards, Hagar and Ishmael are left in the wilderness. Until the coming of Muhammad, the prophets that God sent to humanity for leading us to the righteous path were sent to the Jews, or the Children of Israel.

The descendants of Ishmael, the Arabs, go on to developing their own strange religious beliefs. Arabia was bitterly divided along political lines too during the times of Muhammad. Mecca was ruled by an elite Arab tribe called the Quraish. Incidentally Muhammad himself belonged to this tribe, but he never liked his own family's political and religious practices. He had a challenging childhood. His father Abdullah died before he was even born.

His mother Amina died shortly after he was born. He was mostly raised by his uncle Abu Talib. Muhammad grew up a mysterious kid. At age 25, he married a much older wealthy woman by the name of Khadija who was a merchant.[5] Muhammad often used to retire to a cave in the hills surrounding Mecca and meditate.

One day at age 40, when he was in a cave, he saw what looked to him like an angel of some sort, who asked him to recite a series of words after him. This according to Islamic tradition was the archangel Gabriel, familiar in earlier Jewish and Christian traditions. But Muhammad wasn't sure what had just happened. He went home and told his wife about the experience. She took him to a Christian monk who listened to the whole experience.

The story goes that this monk assured Muhammad he had received a divine revelation from the God of Abraham, Moses and Jesus, the same God whom the Jews and the Christians believed in. This would formally mark the beginnings of Islam as we know it. These revelations kept coming. As Muhammad was himself illiterate, he would memorise the words whispered to him by Gabriel and his followers and disciples would in turn write them down. These words would carry instructions for Muhammad and his followers.

Muhammad came to believe he was the last and final prophet sent to humanity by God. As he began to preach his message, resistance grew from the Quraish tribe of Mecca, the ruling elite, mostly made up of Muhammad's own biological uncles. But his message was strong, and it appealed to many disaffected individuals and groups.

As Muhammad's new movement grew strong, the Quraish tribe felt threatened and came down hard on Muhammad and his followers. Facing stern opposition from the rulers, Muhammad and his early followers decided to migrate to the neighbouring town of Medina to seek refuge. This was a predominantly Jewish neighbourhood. Here Muhammad had a peace treaty with the Jews called the 'Constitution of Medina' signed in 622.[6]

Muhammad's relations with the Jews of Medina were complex. We will deal with this subject in more detail in a later section. All that is important for us to know for now is that as Muhammad's movement grew strong, he found strength in numbers. His passive approach towards the everyday politics back in Mecca changed into one of a statesmen who was prepared to retaliate. Several battles were fought during the course of Muhammad's lifetime. Almost all the religions of Arabia unified under the banner of Islam. His early movement kept getting stronger and eventually succeeded in defeating the ruling Quraish tribe. It ended up conquering the city of Mecca.

Over a period of 23 years, Muhammad had put, not only himself but also the Arabic civilisation in general, on the world map. Shortly after Muhammad's death, Islam soon spread to all ends of the known world at the time. In many respects, the emergence of Islam out of a completely desolate region that had never previously produced a complex civilisation is nothing short of a miracle. Following the birth of Islam, Muhammad's immediate successors went on to conquering significant territory across North Africa, the Middle East, Central Asia and the Subcontinent. Fourteen centuries on, the religion brought to the world by Muhammad now exceeds 1.8 billion followers around the globe.

Differences in Islamic Sects and Teachings

There are two main sects in Islam. The Sunnis, who follow the traditions of the Prophet and his companions, or what one might refer to as his apostles. The Shiites, who draw their practices from the lineage of Muhammad through his daughter Fatima. Like Judaism, Islam is a jurisprudence-based religion. This means that its set of DOs and DON'Ts are numerous as well as deeply complex and often require careful study, analysis and lots of interpretation.

Christianity by comparison is different; it's not legalistic by nature. Christianity is more of a faith-based religion where you must accept that Jesus died for your sins in order to be saved. By comparison, in Judaism and Islam, it isn't sufficient to just believe in the right stuff, it's more so that you have to put into practice the complex set of rites and rituals prescribed by the religion.

Often issues arise that aren't clearly defined in the primary scripture of the religion. For instance, Muslims often debate among themselves whether cigarette smoking is *Halal* (permitted) or *Haram* (prohibited). As tobacco and cigarettes weren't around in the 7th century in Arabia when Islam was born, Islam is naturally silent on the subject. This is a classic case where jurisprudence comes into the picture. Since the religion itself says nothing on the matter, the Muslim jurist or scholar's job would be to see what broader prescriptions one can dig up that may form the basis for providing a *fatwah* (ruling) on the phenomenon in consideration. While I'm no expert on this, I can give an example.

So, a jurist may look at the fact that Islam prohibits the consumption of anything that causes self-harm as well as deliberate waste of money. These two reasons combined cause many jurists to issue a fatwah declaring that cigarette smoking is Haram (prohibited). That's just one out of possibly thousands of examples of how jurisprudence works. It works the same way in Judaism.

Islam has different schools of jurisprudence. In *Sunni* Islam, there are four, each named after a famous Medieval jurist Imam: Hanafi, Maliki, Shafi'i and Hanbali. On top of these, there are fringe groups like the far-left Sufis and far right Salafis also known as Wahhabis. Among Shiite Muslims, there are three main schools of thought: Ithna-Asharis, Ismailis and Zaidis.

There are also the Ibadhis of Oman, a unique sect that is neither Sunni nor Shiite. Historically there were other groups such as the Mu'tazilites and Kharijites that have died out over time. While the sectarian and denominational divisions within Christianity can range from theological to doctrinal reasons, for the most part, the sectarian divisions within Islam have less to do with theology and more to do with politics and jurisprudence.

What does Islam mean for today's world?

Islam is unique as a religion. There is a reason for this. As discussed earlier, Judaism is legalistic, but not evangelical. Christianity is evangelical, but not legalistic. Islam is both legalistic and evangelical at the same time. This means Islam not only has a desire to reach out to the rest of the world, it also requires a jurisdiction where its laws could be implemented as state policy.

Remember, we talked about how Islam had its own set of civil and criminal laws? Well, it follows that unless Islam is the dominant force in each territory, those laws could not be implemented. We will deal in greater deal with Islam's laws, called *Sharia*, later in the book. All that's necessary at this stage is to get our heads around this concurrently legalistic and evangelical nature of the religion. It is precisely this nature that makes it impossible in Islam to separate what we in the West have come to understand as the separation between the Church and the State. It must be said at this point that by 'church' we are not simply referring to the building Christians go to worship at on Sundays. That's the other use of the term Church.

In this context, Church means the whole institution and organisation of Christian clergy. State means the political body that rules over us; the country, nation-state, or the Kingdom depending on where one lives. During the Middle Ages in Europe, there used to be no separation between the Church and the State. The Pope, who was head of the Church, was often either the head of the state at the same time or held final authority over the King or Queen who was the head of the state. The Church could tax its population, raise revenue, sanction a war among dozens of other powers which we, in the modern world, would associate with the state, but not the church.

The invention of the printing press was a major turning point in European history.[7] Starting in the 1450s, Europe discovered a way to print books in large quantities. This meant that education, which was previously only given to the scholastics, the priests and the nobles, had to now be given to ordinary peasants and farmers. Books would be printed *en masse* and circulated throughout Europe. The Bible, which was previously read in either Latin or Greek and only understood by priests with specialised language training, now began to be translated into local languages of German, English and French. People in those parts of Europe felt more empowered than ever before.

An almost immediate consequence of the Print Revolution was the Protestant Reformation starting in 1517.[8] It began as a protest against the authority of the Catholic Church and was very much a direct result of the rise of literacy and scripture being translated in the same timeframe.

As people were able to read the Bible in their local languages with proper understanding, they could now identify that many of the practices of the Church were not sanctioned within the Christian scripture but were innovations created by the Church. As the Church's authority came under heavy criticism with grassroots revolts, Europe entered into a phase of long and bloody conflicts between the Catholics and the Protestants that lasted well over a century and a half, coming to a halt in roughly 1648 with the signing of the Treaty of Westphalia.[9]

As a result of these upheavals, combined with the emergence of The Age of Enlightenment and its philosophy, the authority of the Church began to diminish over time. There was no clear date that serves as a single turning point when the separation of the Church and the State took place in Christian Europe.

This so-called separation was a long and violent process. It literally took centuries to get it right. Arguably when the United States of America emerged on the world map on 4th July 1776,[10] it officially became the world's first country to neither have a religious head of church like a pope, nor a political head of state like a king or queen who would rule by divine right. Ruling by consent of the people is itself a key feature of the separation of church and state.[11]

Early colonial American society was highly influenced by both the Protestant Reformation and Enlightenment philosophy. That's why it's hardly surprising that when America finally got its independence from the British Empire, it didn't opt to become a monarchy like the rest of Europe at the time.

It would have made no sense to first defeat a monarch, King George III of England, only to then appoint its own King George Washington of America. Imagine that! It would have been a case of replacing one monarchy with another. Washington was all for democracy and opted to conduct the first democratic elections and became the first President of the United States of America in 1789.[12] Democracy was now on the world map. As time went on, the rest of Europe and eventually most of the world either have removed its monarchy or reduced its rights to interfere in the everyday politics in their respective societies. This is generally called Constitutional Monarchy. Australia is a prime example of this.

While we have Queen Elizabeth II as our Head of State, she does not interfere in governing Australia. The governance side of things is handled by the Prime Minister, our Head of Government, and the Parliament, which comprises politicians who are elected by the people.

Islam has always aspired to spread itself to the rest of the world. Shortly following Prophet Muhammad's death, Islam managed to expand geographically from Spain in the east to China in the west. In those days, warfare was the norm. Virtually every culture and civilisation exercised the use of force to acquire more territory and expand beyond its own borders.

Take a look at the Vikings for instance and the amount of land they conquered across Scandinavia and Western Europe around the exact same timeframe. We'd be incorrect to presume Islamic civilisation was the only one expanding territory by use of force. In fact, long before Islam there were complex warring civilisations in Greece, Rome, Persia and India. If anything, the Arabs were quite late in coming to the party and building their own expansionist empire. Yet as time has gone on, especially from World War II onwards, nations of the world have gradually shifted away from resolving disputes by means of warfare, as well as from acquiring new lands through war. All cultures and nations of the world got away with conquering their fair share of lands and expanding their empires beyond their points of origin in that old-world order.

This doesn't just include Arabs or Muslims; it literally includes all developed cultures of the world. If we are going to start criticising Islam for its colonial conquests, we would have to start criticising every other culture and civilisation including Christian Europe for conquering so much land and hoisting its flag wherever it could. The fact is that nobody broke any rules by conquering territory because that, prior to World War II, was normal practice. Although this isn't to say that the road ahead for the Islamic world is free from challenge.[13]

As Islam has its own civil and criminal laws requiring its own jurisdiction, this makes it an inherently political religion. It is not a religion where you can simply switch off the politics of the day and reduce the authority of the religion into something like a symbolic Vatican City style arrangement. Or at least, such a thing has not yet proven possible.

The Vatican City, although still a theocratic state, does not have the capacity to sanction war. Much of what we know as the Islamic world today was colonised by a European power in the last 500 years or so. Although there are exceptions such as Turkey, Iran and Afghanistan. Much of the rest of Muslim countries on the world map across North Africa and the Middle East came under French, British or Italian colonial rule.

Much of Central Asia came under Soviet control. Much of South and Southeast Asia was predominantly under British, Portuguese or Dutch rule.

Before the rise of European imperialism, like the rest of the world, these regions of the Islamic world were ruled by monarchies. They were territorially expansionist empires.

In the world of Islam, there was never an event remotely like the Protestant Reformation of Europe, let alone The Age of Enlightenment. If anything, the world of Islam has gone backwards from being more tolerant during its short-lived Golden Age to being less tolerant in the centuries that followed.

As those Muslim countries began to gain independence during the early to mid-1900s, they couldn't simply go back to govern their affairs through the laws of Islam under a Sharia Law based on the caliphate system. As the West itself went through various political reforms and that separation of Church and State occurred, it passed down these ideas into its colonies.

So much of the Islamic countries that emerged on the world map after the process of decolonisation have tended to be modelled on some sort of hybrid system that inherits secular institutions from the West. For instance, an independent judiciary, parliaments, political parties and elections, an independent bureaucracy and a non-political defence force on the one hand, and elements of Islamic social norms such as various blasphemy laws or laws concerning inheritance, marriage and divorce from traditional Islam on the other.

From Morocco all the way to Indonesia, there is not one Muslim country today that practices Sharia Law the way Islam's founder intended for it to be practiced. There are some countries that implement aspects of Sharia Law, some more so than others. Yet the world can't simply go back to live as a caliphate in this day and age because the rules have changed. Unless, of course, if it was based on the Vatican model. You can no longer wage expansionist warfare, especially not in a nuclear age. Since none of the governments of the 57 Muslim majority nations of the world is a proper and precise example of the ideal Islamic government with Sharia Law, this absence of a caliphate has become a prime reason for the fundamentalists and terrorists to start urging Muslims to do what they can to establish a caliphate through armed struggle.

So, the idea that terrorism is happening in the world due to American-led military intervention in Muslim lands only works up to a certain point. Yes it's true those invasions don't help, they alienate large numbers of people and kill civilians while breeding further hatred of America, but at the same time, one can't ignore the fact various regions of the Islamic world have ended up dealing with fundamentalism and terrorism even in times of no American-led intervention whatsoever.

The Americans took a backseat following the end of the Soviet-Afghan War in 1989. That region got exactly what many Muslims today suggest America should do, i.e. to pull right back and not police the region. The end result of the American withdrawal was the rise of the Taliban who by 1996 had taken over most of the country. The end result was September 11, 2001. This resulted in another two wars, the War on Terror in Afghanistan and subsequently the war in Iraq.

We see time and again, there have been constant struggles within the Islamic world between moderate Muslims who simply want to go about their daily lives and their fundamentalist counterparts that are constantly struggling to install a theocratic state, a Sunni caliphate, on the world map.

Moving forwards, the real challenge for Islam is whether, like Christianity, it can experience its own separation of the Church and the State and find a way to reconcile its traditional values with liberal democratic politics. The Western world has certainly been able to pull this off, albeit after centuries of struggle.

The question is, can Islamic civilisation do the same? This is a question every young Muslim should be thinking about long and hard. What sort of an Islamic society do we wish to live in? Through education and exposure, one can only hope that the fanatical obsession some have with the idea of re-establishing some sort of a caliphate will vanish over time. Either that, or if the Islamic world could have its own Vatican City style 'symbolic' caliphate.

Although the trouble with that idea is that Christianity is not legalistic, so you can have something like the Vatican. But Islam is legalistic, it would be a real struggle to imagine an Islam without a jurisdiction and Sharia Law. And then we have the varying interpretations of Sharia Law due to jurisprudential differences. It is time for modern Muslim scholars to clarify the details of Sharia Law in relation to an Islamic state, and if necessary, reform it from within. The simple fact is, since World War II, we can no longer afford to have theocratic states with the power to commission a war because, let's face it, battles are no longer fought on the back of horses and chariots carrying swords and shields. Nor are they fought on the battlefield between professional warriors and knights. With weapons of mass destruction in existence, humanity is now at a junction where we could literally blow ourselves out of existence if there was another large-scale world war. The question is, can Islamic civilisation still play by the rules of the 21st century and remain a relevant force in guiding the lives of its 1.8 billion adherents around the world.

I for one am optimistic that the Islamic world can reform and get the balance right. That's why it's important for us to keep this conversation going and this book is a humble attempt to do precisely that.

3

Myths and Facts I: Islam and Politics

People can't be blamed for thinking that Islam by its nature is a political religion. The extent to which this might be true has already been discussed when we looked at Islam's basic history and development. Often the way people in the West hear about Islam in the news doesn't really help paint a particularly favourable image of the religion.

As with any other topic of public interest, it goes without saying there are certain things which the public believes about Islam and politics that are true and things that are not. The same is the case with any ideology. Ask any staunch capitalist, socialist, Christian or Buddhist if in their view everything that everyone else believes about their beliefs is accurate or not, and the answer will likely be an emphatic no.

This is primarily because there is usually more to a story than what randomly lands in our news feed on social media. If an ISIS video showing a journalist being beheaded goes viral on the internet, most people can't be blamed if they don't have the time, interest nor critical thinking ability to go and properly research authentic

Islam and find out whether its teachings are actually violent or not. The truth is that in English-speaking Western culture, people barely pay much attention to their own history and religion, let alone trying to understand someone else's. As a proud Australian Muslim, I see it as my job to clear away misconceptions to the best of my understanding. There's a lot of ground to cover and while this book won't have all the answers for you, its aim is to go further than most people have.

What follows from here on is a series of comprehensive responses to the frequently asked questions that have been thrown at me through my interaction with non-Muslims daily, especially on my Facebook page. These are all valid questions and deserve a response. My intention in answering these is to give you simple, straightforward, no-nonsense responses based on facts and evidence.

It's my sincere hope that reading through my responses below will ignite your curiosity and to further it enough so that you are curious to familiar yourself with Islam, not the way the media portrays it, but the way most Muslims experience it as a living, breathing, vibrant faith that continues to guide 1.8 billion people around the world.

Is the Separation of Church and State Possible in Islam?

Before diving into any discussion as to whether or not a separation between the Church and the State is possible in Islam, it is crucial to shed some light on what these terms mean and why discussing such a separation with respect to Islam is even important in the first place. I will begin with the very basics.

We all know that a *State* is the political jurisdiction within which you live. Australia is a state. It's called the Commonwealth of Australia. In another sense New South Wales is also a state within

Australia. Australia is a sovereign *nation-state*, meaning an actual country whereas New South Wales, while still a subordinate state, falls within the jurisdiction of the Commonwealth of Australia. In other words, a province of some sort.

When we speak of a *Church* however, this is where it gets a bit trickier because that can mean one of two things. In one sense, a church is a Christian place of worship in the same way that a Synagogue is a Jewish place of worship, or a Mosque a Muslim place of worship, or a Temple a Hindu or Buddhist place of worship. Talking about a church in this sense is merely a reference to the physical structure; the building within which a community of Christians may congregate at the Sunday mass to worship.

In the other sense, a church is an institution, much like an organisation with its own hierarchy, membership and clergy. The expression 'Separation of Church and State' obviously refers to a church in this second sense. Although you would be surprised at the staggering number of people who not only end up confused, they also start referring to expressions such as 'Separation of Mosque and State' without realising that unlike the case with Christianity, in Islam a Mosque is only a church in the first sense, i.e. a place of worship where Muslims congregate. There is no religious institution within Islam comparable to the Catholic Church.

As discussed earlier, Christianity broke away from Judaism sometime around the first and second centuries of the Common Era and later developed into an independent religion, with its own beliefs and institutions. While Christianity is more of a personal and spiritual religion without a legal code like the *Halacha* of Judaism or *Sharia* of Islam, as it came to be adopted by the Roman Empire as its state religion under Emperor Theodosius I in 381 AD[14], it not only evolved into a religious institution, it also became a political institution that would go on to struggle to find the right balance between religious authority and political authority for more than a thousand years to come.

While in our times, the Pope in the Vatican only represents religious authority but not political authority; this hasn't always been the case. For much of history, a Pope had the power to create and repeal laws much like the institution of the Parliament does in our times. A Pope could levy a tax or commission a war - and often did so. For most of Christian European history, from the early to the late Middle Ages, the State that is the embodiment of political authority was governed by a King or Queen under a feudal system while the Church that is the embodiment of religious authority was governed by the Pope. Often there were intense tensions between the two.

If a King or Queen did not like a particular Pope, they would interfere in the internal politics of the Church and attempt to have him replaced with one that was more in line with the monarchy's interests. The same often happened in reverse; if a particular Pope didn't get along with a King or Queen, they would seek to have their authority overruled. One example most people can relate to would be the tensions between King Henry VIII and the Church because he wanted to divorce and remarry which wasn't allowed at the time, so he broke off to set up his own quasi-religious political authority which eventually became the Church of England.[15]

Popes were able to wage war during the Middle Ages, and too often they did just that. A classic example is Pope Urban II's famous edict *Inter Gracias* that called for a Europe-wide Crusade against the Jews and Muslims in 1095 to gain control over Jerusalem.[16] The thought of the current Pope Francis calling for, say the invasion of Iraq would make global headlines and be met with mass criticism from the public. Yet this was the norm only a few centuries ago.

Not only did the Church, in the second sense, wield too much authority for its own good in those times, there was also the issue of controlling knowledge, that is, what could and could not be expressed publicly. To maintain its own authority, the Church suppressed freedom of thought and expression. A classic example is when Galileo first proposed that it's not the sun that revolves around the earth but rather the earth goes around the sun; this created a great controversy for the Church.[17]

You might rightfully wonder who cares what one guy believes about the sun and the earth, why should the Church be concerned? The issue was that all metaphysical knowledge about nature, being and reality was entwined with religious knowledge. People tended to defer to the judgement of the Church hierarchy to learn about nature rather than making their own observations using critical thinking.

In those times, the idea that the sun was the centre of the universe and everything else revolved around it was an established belief and for Galileo to turn up and argue that's false was too big a hit for the authority of the church. This is only one of literally thousands of such cases. Popes often banned literature and burnt alive the philosopher who came up with theories that contradicted established belief authorised by the Church. This continued to be the case both before and after the Reformation in 1517.

Pope Urban II commissioning a war, King Henry VIII being unable to divorce and remarry as he wished and Galileo being persecuted for coming up with an alternative theory about the solar system, are three of literally thousands of similar cases of tensions between the Church and the State. It's not really surprising that Europe eventually ended up going through a long and violent process following the Protestant Reformation in 1517 and The Age of Enlightenment from 1600s to 1750s that ended up shrinking the authority of the Catholic Church and led to a complete separation of the Church and the State.

Yet it wasn't just the religious authority of the Catholic Church that took a hit during this process. The political authority of Kings and Queens took an even greater hit. Remember that during the Middle Ages, Kings and Queens didn't seek people's approval to govern them; they did so usually based on the idea of a Divine Right. That is, the idea that Kings and Queens ruled over people because God wills them to.

A monarchy was usually established after a war. Someone invades a territory, either the existing King or Queen surrenders or gets killed by the invader and the invader then sets up his or her own dynasty. The descendants from the dynasty would remain Kings and Queen until someone else comes along, challenges their authority and defeats them in war. That was the old-world order.

By the time of the American Revolution in 1776 and the French Revolution in 1789, not only was it the idea of a separation between church and state that had already set itself in stone, the idea of Divine Right also took a massive hit. Due to the widespread influence of Enlightenment philosophy, people were no longer prepared to accept that anyone could rule over them without their consent. The American and the French revolutions became the pioneering examples of the birth of ruling by consent.

When American rebel leader George Washington defeated King George III of the ruling British Empire, he could have declared himself as the first King of America and set up his own dynasty as the case was across most of Europe. Instead, he opted for presidential elections so that people could forever continue to choose who their leader should be. One might go so far as to say that if it wasn't for that, America might well have turned out to be a monarchy and had it not shown the rest of the world the way to democracy, we could well have still been living in the Middle Ages.

By this stage you should have a good idea of how and why the separation of Church and State occurred within Christianity. It is because these especially important details are too often left out of the public discussion, people struggle to take a position on whether Islam requires some sort of a separation between its religious and political authorities. Having understood the context within the Christian case, let's now turn our focus to the Islamic case.

As previously discussed, unlike Christianity, Islam does have its own legal system called the Sharia Law. This means that in a sense, religious and political authorities are inseparable in Islam. If you didn't have a territory to rule, how else would you enforce Sharia Law? Islam began as both a religious and political movement in its day. By the end of the 23 years of Prophet Muhammad's career or ministry as a prophet, him and his followers had conquered the entire Arabian Peninsula and shortly after his death, the caliphs who succeeded him went on to conquering even more territory as far west as Spain and as far east as China.

While Islam institutionalised political authority in the form of a state, oddly it does not institutionalise religious authority.[18] Islamic jurisprudence works on a principle of consensus a bit like the academic community. At what point do people in the scientific community know whether a particular theory has legs or not? A scientist publishes a paper, it goes through the peer-review process, if the small community of those in the know look at it and majority among them want to give it the green light it gets published and is accepted as valid. Then a challenger comes along to argue a different case and goes through the same peer review process.

Islamic jurisprudence works the same way. There are multiple sects and schools of thought but authority, at least in Sunni Islam, is not institutionalised in the form of something like a papacy. The case with Shi'ite Islam is a bit different, in that they do have a form of papacy, which is what Ayatollah Khomeini re-established in Iran during the 1979 Revolution.[19]

So, Iran in this sense is a theocratic state where religious authority rests in the supreme Ayatollah while political authority rests in the President and Prime Ministers that are elected by popular vote. In the case of Sunni Islam, throughout history there was never a single caliphate, often there were multiple caliphates in different parts of the world, and this generally worked.[20]

As a relatively recent example, the Ottoman Empire ruled over much of the Mediterranean world and the Arabian Peninsula the same time as the Mughal Empire ruled over the Subcontinent. The Islamic world also went through its share of tensions between political authority vested in the caliph and religious authority vested in the collective body of *ulama* or scholars of Islam, think of it as the peer-review community without a formal structure. Often if a caliph did not like a particular religious scholar, he would have them trialled or imprisoned, not dissimilar in nature to European history.

Yet it must be noted that since political authority in Islam was formal while religious authority was not, the struggles between the two weren't as pronounced as the case was in Europe. Remember that in Europe both the monarchy and the papacy could pretty much operate like a state. They could levy taxes; they could start a war and they could summon someone to a trial and subsequent imprisonment. In Islam's case, the ulama or the scholars have never had that level of power, only the state did, that is the caliphate.

So, in a sense, it may be said that the case of the Islamic world is the exact inverse of the case with Europe. Now in the West, there exists a clear divide between religious and political authorities. The Vatican is simply a symbolic theocracy that does not have its own military and it exists within Italy as an institution that does not interfere in the political affairs of the world. The Pope can no longer call for a war.

In Islam's case, through an entirely organic process, it's not the religious authority that was cornered like it was in the West's case; it was political authority that was abolished. With the fall of the Ottoman Empire at the end of World War II, there has not been a single Sunni caliphate anywhere in the world.[21] There are 57 Muslim nations in the world. Not even one of them is a Sunni caliphate.

While this fact may not bother most Muslims, it does bother a minority within the scholarship of Islam. Therefore, a difference of opinions exists among these scholars about how a caliphate can be achieved. You have those who say the strategy should be to become part of the existing democratic structures, form Islamic political parties, run a campaign and get voted in by a popular vote then declare a caliphate. The most recent example of this was in Egypt after the Arab Spring when the Muslim brotherhood took power under Muhammad Morsi.[22]

The other means is through asymmetric warfare, or what everyone understands as terrorism. This is the mentality adopted by the Taliban, Al-Qaeda and ISIS. It is perfectly understandable why so many wonder whether a separation between church and state is possible in Islam, because when we see things from a Western point of view, the convergence between religious and political authorities never truly worked for us in European history. Hence one institution had to be separated from another.

In Islam's case, religious authority as discussed isn't even an institution of its own, political authority is, and currently there is no caliphate anywhere in the world. The governments of the vast majority of the 57 Muslim nations around the world are based on a range of different models. Pakistan for instance is a Westminster Parliamentary democracy with elements of Sharia Law thrown in.[23] It has a bicameral Parliament, there are political parties, there is a free press, elections are held after every term and people vote for their leader which is exactly like our own system in Australia.

Yet at the same time, Pakistan has its infamous blasphemy law which is the Sharia Law element thrown into the equation.[24] Saudi Arabia on the other hand is an absolute monarchy with a heavy degree of Sharia Law.[25] Yet it still doesn't count as a caliphate because the ruler comes from a monarchic system. In an ideal caliphate, the leader would be chosen by the ulama or scholars. So, the short answer to our broader question is, Church and State in Islam do not mean what people might think they mean. We keep understanding Islam through a Christian lens, because political and religious authorities clashed in European history until they had to be divorced, we expect the same from Islam.

Due to Islam's institutional lack of religious authority, i.e. lack of Pope, religious scholars can work in tandem with the political order of the day. The people trying to establish a caliphate through popular vote like the Muslim brotherhood or through terrorism like ISIS are a minority. They need to realise that these methods were not and are not prescribed within Islam.

Just as in early Islam, you had the Ottomans ruling the Mediterranean and the Mughals ruling the Subcontinent at the same time without trying to create a single confederated Islamic State, in today's world each of the 57 Muslim nations and their governments need to be understood as caliphates in their own right. The religious scholarship must respect their authority and work in tandem, rather than trying to be subversive. For the most part, the mainstream scholarship already does understand this, but there is a small minority that does not. Rather, they exploit the idea of a caliphate for political gain and that is something none of us should tolerate.

Does Islam condone violence and terrorism?

We live in anxious times. Hardly a day goes by without coming across news headlines that report on suicide attacks or beheadings somewhere around the globe. I have made the point repeatedly, while it's true that not all Muslims are terrorists, who could deny that in this day and age, almost all terrorists are Muslims. This is as much a problem for Westerners as it is for Muslims. Westerners don't want their comfort and security to be disrupted by some crazy lunatic when all they're trying to do is to go about their daily lives peacefully. Neither do ordinary Muslims want a crazy lunatic to commit these barbaric acts in the name of their religion, because this causes backlash against the wider Islamic community.

Practically every informed citizen who keeps an eye on the news has heard of famous terrorist incidents in recent decades. The World Trade Centre attacks in New York on September 11, the Bali Bombings, the London and Madrid attacks, the Boston Marathon

Bombings and the Sydney Siege to name a few. The Bali Bombings hold a special place in the Australian psyche not only because of how close to home it happened, but largely due to the fact that it killed 202 people simply trying to have fun at a nightclub, not hurting anyone, and 88 of those were Australians.[26] The same goes for the Sydney Siege. It was a case of ordinary people trying to grab a coffee on their way to work, held at ransom for hours against their will, by a crazy Muslim fanatic.

It's true that Muslims don't like it when people think that Islam allows terrorism and while they're right in a strict sense, people cannot be blamed for thinking that Islam and terrorism are correlated. We must cut the average person some slack here. It is perfectly understandable to ask whether Islam is a religion that permits violence and terrorism. Before we delve into this question, it is important to acknowledge that different societies have different thresholds for the tolerance of violence.

One glance at local newspapers across North Africa and the Middle East illustrates this. Images of dead people often drenched in blood can be extremely confronting for Western audiences. We don't like violence, except in movies and video games, and we certainly don't like seeing actual pictures of dead or grossly injured people. These are not published in our newspapers and if they were, there would be a backlash from the readership against their publication.

Yet in Middle Eastern culture, kids from a young age are accustomed to seeing their dads and uncles slitting the throat of an animal at *Eid al-Adha* once a year. The streets of major Muslim capitals around the world from Casablanca to Jakarta are drenched in fresh red blood on the day of Eid al-Adha from all the animal sacrifices that are carried out on a large scale.

So, people are used to seeing blood, and dead bodies cut up in those regions. They are culturally accustomed and desensitised to that. The same is not true of Westerners. We are not used to seeing wounds, scars or anything of that sort beyond the realm of cinema. Nor are we accustomed to political violence. It is true that Western political history is incredibly violent, but the modern age is not. In English-speaking West societies, people do not witness much violence on the street in any shape or form on a daily basis. The rare times that violence is witnessed in Western culture it is called out for what it is in the media.

Often when terrorist incidents happen in the West and the media starts speculating about the role of Islam, Muslims get offended and start alleging that you're singling them out. Too often we see Muslim leaders coming out and trying to point out that the number one victim of terrorism are Muslims themselves. This is certainly true if we consider all the violence that Muslim terrorists inflict on other Muslims within Islamic countries, but the violence inflicted on civilians by Muslim terrorists in Western countries is almost always directed at non-Muslims.

So, mentioning to Westerners that Muslims are the number one victims of Islamic terrorism, even if true, won't win you any friends. It's not a way to show empathy to the Western victims of Islamic terrorism. This is something leaders of the Muslim community across Western nations need to work on. Besides, when those terrorist attacks happen in, say, Baghdad or Peshawar within the Islamic world, remember my point about the threshold for violence and bloodshed.

It almost becomes part of the daily routine to subconsciously accept that these incidents are now part and parcel of the political environment. People in the Islamic world therefore have a different threshold. We in the West aren't used to such chaos and instability. It would be grossly unjust to suddenly expect the West to be accustomed to such extreme violence.

We will not be accepting terrorism as part and parcel of our daily lives. We will not be lowering our threshold on how much blood and violence our eyes can cope with seeing. This is precisely why I was extremely disappointed with the Mayor of London, Mr Sadiq Khan when he said that being prepared for terrorism was part and parcel of life in a city like London.[27] Such comments are foolish, insensitive and more damaging to the perception of Muslims in the West than anything else.

Although the question as to whether Islam is itself a violent religion or not has never been more important, it must also be kept in mind there are two forms of violence that have tarnished Islam's global image, especially in the eyes of Westerners. One is the overly harsh punishments prescribed by Islam. The other is the incitement to violence and suicide attacks for political reasons.

Often when critics talk about Islam being a violent religion, this distinction isn't clearly drawn. The discussion usually ends up failing to properly address the issue. Let's first start by discussing Islam's punishment methods. Many Westerners are concerned that Islam prescribes that the hands of a thief be chopped off, or that the head of the murderer be cut off, or that unmarried fornicators be lashed publicly while married adulterers who cheat on their partners be stoned to death.

As Islam is based on Judaism, it inherits many of the punishments prescribed within the Torah, that is the first five books of the Old Testament which both Jews and Christians accept as valid. Whether we're talking about Judaism or Islam, one has to bear in mind these religions are products of totally different timeframes. Their prescribed norms were too often shaped by completely different social realities. Today we have more education and awareness, we have evolved modern technology, we are more civilised and advanced. Most punishments in the West revolve around issuing monetary fines or a jail sentence, none of which sheds blood or causes any physical harm. There are exceptions in some jurisdictions within the United States where the death penalty still applies,[28] but it is fair to say that most of the Western world has moved right past violent punishments.

Remember that the point of a punishment is more than seeking retribution or justice for the doing wrong. Equally importantly, punishment is about deterrence. Crimes are not always committed in isolation from society but within societies and have an ongoing impact on the overall health and well-being of the given society. For instance, we know that if you rob a bank or murder another civilian except in self-defence, chances are you'll go to jail for life.

Since this awareness exists on a large scale due to our education system and mass media, the government does not need to come up with a way of frightening us to obey the law. In ancient societies where there was less education and technology, this option wasn't so readily available. So, when we look back at ancient legal systems, even outside of Judaism and Islam, we find that everywhere in the world, the penalties for committing even the pettiest of crimes were often incredibly harsh, not just in our eyes as modern observers, but even by the relative standards of those times.

The Code of Hammurabi in ancient Babylonia is a case in point.[29] Much of the beheadings and stoning's for doing the smallest thing wrong, such as stealing a loaf of bread, are found within it. Ancient Judaism, which serves as the prototype for Islam, is not at all unlike the rest of the legal systems prevalent within the ancient Middle East. Remember the point that in those days, the easiest way to deter your citizens from committing a crime was by coming up with an incredibly harsh method of punishment for the one person that had committed the crime and then displaying the same publicly. This practice would strike fear in people's hearts and was a strategy that worked well for centuries.

Surveying methods of punishment in Medieval Europe during the peak period of Christian rule shows us how the Catholic Church used to have all sorts of punishment methods most Catholics today would not have a clue about. None of this information is generally taught in Catholic schools. For instance, people's nails were often ripped out, their bodies tied to a wooden plank, drawn and quartered, people were often thrown alive into a boiling well of water, people were castrated and even literary critics were often burnt at the stake with the literature that they wrote only because their views differed from those of the Church.[30]

I for one do not believe these methods of punishment were an eternal reflection on Christianity nor the Catholic Church. This was a product of its time and should be treated as such. Perhaps in the Medieval Era if they had the Internet and smartphones combined with a democratic society with modern education available at their disposal, the Catholic Church too would have been issuing simple fines and prison sentences. This is the framework within which the overly harsh punishments of Sharia Law need to be interpreted.

Be that as it may, there is another little-known fact about Sharia Law that is too often left out of any conversation on the subject, this has been comprehensively covered in another section of this book that deals with Sharia Law in detail. The point is, for anyone to be properly convicted of a crime in a Sharia court, there must be a Caliphate first. If there is no Caliphate and there are no Sharia courts, then those punishments do not apply, and the law of the land suffices.

If, however the crime occurs within a Caliphate, even then, you cannot simply convict somebody based on mere allegation or empty accusations. This is because the burden of proof in Islam is much tougher than the burden of proof in Common Law and Civil Law systems. For instance, you cannot simply lodge a complaint in an authentic Sharia court and allege that someone had sexual intercourse outside of wedlock. Unless, there were four adult practising Muslim males prepared to testify in a trial confirming that all four of them had seen with their own eyes the act of penetration.[31]

Given the extremely high improbability of someone having sexual intercourse being seen in the act by four adult practising Muslim males, chances are that if Sharia Law was applied correctly as has been prescribed, nobody would end up being punished in the first instance. Once we come to terms with these realities, we end up realising that Islam is not the horribly violent religion so many have come to think it is. It is worth noting that the burden of proof works in a similar way in Jewish law in Halachic courts.[32]

It is fair to wonder whether, if that's how Sharia law is truly supposed to work, how do we end up with all those cases that make global headlines? We've seen women shot in the back of the head by the Taliban some two decades ago or the more recent case of Asia Bibi in Pakistan that very nearly ended up being killed for blasphemy.

For starters, Pakistan is not a strictly Sharia abiding country. It is primarily a Westminster parliamentary democracy like Australia itself, with a bicameral Parliament and political parties and it conducts elections after every term. What it does have though, is elements of Sharia law interwoven into the country's Common law system. Often these elements are implemented and enforced incorrectly. Often, lesser-educated farmers in rural Pakistan evoke the country's controversial blasphemy law enshrined in its Constitution Section 295C to get even with members of Christian minorities. This is obviously not ideal, but it doesn't happen due to Islam. It happens due to the incorrect implementation of Islam.

The same is true of Brunei, Iran, Afghanistan and some other countries that practice whole or parts of the Sharia Law. The important point is, there is more to Sharia Law than simply chopping off people's body parts. As previously discussed, the whole system is based on evidentiary requirements that are so strict by their very nature that if implemented correctly, they would almost never be satisfied. How odd would it be for a couple having sex to let four adult practising males see them?

How odd would it have to be for a gay couple doing their thing to allow for adult practising males to see them in the act? Some of these countries that have hybrid legal systems often ignore the evidentiary requirements. Why? Because they inherit the punishment itself from the Sharia, but the evidentiary requirements from their Common or Civic Law systems and that's where a large part of the problem lies. No doubt, Sharia Law is a product of its time and its harsh penalties were designed to deter other potential offenders from committing crimes in an age when education and literacy were lacking.

As far as the idea that Islam condones terrorism is concerned, this is false. Islam neither encourages nor condones terrorism in any shape or form. Most of the violent tactics used by Islamist terrorist organisations are borrowed from 20th century nationalist or separatist movements, such as the Bolsheviks, the Irish Republican Army (IRA) or Tamil Tigers. These tactics are not prescribed by authentic Islam.

There is a common perception among critics that Muslims aren't doing enough to condemn terrorism. While it's true that a lot of celebrity Muslims in the West often condemn terrorism in an evasive way as if they don't mean it, we mustn't forget that most of these prominent Muslims aren't well versed in Islamic jurisprudence.

While I'm not either, I was fortunate enough to have had the kind of upbringing that taught me enough to know the truth and the difference between right and wrong. I know that many prominent and authentic scholars of Islam in its mainstream form have issued rulings to condemn terrorism. Sheikh Muhammad Tahir-ul-Qadri is a leading Pakistani cleric and renowned across the Muslim world for publishing his extensive 600-page fatwah against suicide terrorism.[33]

His fatwah was officially endorsed by the most eminent Islamic university in the world, Al-Azhar University in Cairo. The same fatwah also ruled against forcing Islam on other people. Likewise, Sheikh Abdul Aziz Al-Sheikh, the Grand Mufti of Saudi Arabia issued a fatwah after the London bombings in 2005 and said "Killing and terrorising innocent people and the destruction of property are not condoned by Islam".[34] As we can see, Islam neither condones violence nor terrorism.

Do suicide bombers really get 72 virgins in heaven?

Among the most frequently laid charges against Islam in our times is that it incentivises suicide bombers by promising sex with virgins in heaven. Again, this is not the Islam my mother taught me, nor the Islam of the average Muslim household. But I guess the best way to approach this is by pointing out the obvious, remember that most organised religions are based on their fair share of allegories, parables and other mythical content, which is not to be taken literally. When the Christian New Testament, for instance, promises that believers will sit on the "right hand side of God"[35] does this imply that God actually has a pair of hands? Or when Jews and Christians both believe that God created the heavens, the earth and all life within it in six days and took a rest on the seventh day[36] hence the Sabbath as the day of rest, does this imply 24-hour days like ours?

How could there be 24 hour days when a 'day' depends not only on the existence of the sun as the source of light, but also on the earth rotating on its own axis so as to create the illusion of daylight and night time darkness, yet the Bible tells us that the sun and the earth weren't created till day four? Who knows? Add to this the Armageddon prophecies in the New Testament that talk about the four horsemen in the book of Revelation.[37] There is widespread debate whether these are mere allegorical references or actual literal references pointing to things in physical reality.

My point here is that nearly all organised religions have a mythical dimension. People don't always think of it that way, but if we're being true to ourselves, that's more or less what it is. That dimension is a realm where the laws of physics and other earthly normalities do not apply. It's a fairy-tale world of fantasy, miracles and magic. In that realm, Moses can part the Red Sea,[38] Jesus can turn water into wine[39] and the Prophet Muhammad can ascend into heaven on the back of a horse with wings.[40] Saying that such beliefs belong to the mythical realm does not altogether dismiss their validity. It simply only says there is a high chance these stories are of an allegorical nature, and the less literalist an approach we take when interpreting them, the better.

Without bearing this in mind, we cannot proceed to discussing this subject of 72 virgins. It is certainly true that there are hadiths that mention that pious Muslim men will be rewarded with virgins in heaven. But there is widespread debate among scholars whether Islam prescribes a physical heaven, or a spiritual one. While these hadiths talking about 72 virgins exist, there are two crucial points to bear in mind here. Firstly, most mainstream scholars have tended to interpret them in a metaphorical way. Secondly, the vast majority of Muslims don't even know these hadiths exist. Often, the critics of Islam know more about this "72 virgins in heaven" idea than actual Muslims. Isn't that funny? Just the same way that anti-Semites seem to know more about Jews running the world than actual Jews.

This is because terrorist organisations have exploited these allegories and metaphors to pry on the desperate and recruit them by offering these 72 virgins in heaven as an incentive for causing suicide bombing. If this whole idea of dying for 72 virgins were officially mandated for men in authentic Islam, you'd think that our mum would've brought it up at dinnertime conversations with my brothers.

Bear in mind that if someone was to make stuff up about the Jewish or Christian religions, the instant response from mainstream members within those communities would be that "that's not the Judaism I was taught" and "this isn't the Christianity I was raised to believe in" and nobody, for half a second, would bat an eyelid. Nobody would, for instance, dare to tell a Jew or a Christian "But wait a minute, I know your religion better than you know it yourself". Yet this continuously happens to mainstream Muslims, trying to follow a peaceful and authentic version of Islam as taught to them by their parents. I, included.

We must be cautious never to allow the terrorist to turn something from the mythical dimension of Islam into an object of physical reality. That is exactly what the extremist wants, and we don't want to be helping them push ahead with their divisive agenda. So, if we, as the critics and sceptics of Islam in the West, keep telling those moderate voices that your religion really is about dying for 72 virgins in heaven, then I don't see how we are helping solve the situation.

Sharia Law: What it is and what it's not

There is no shortage of stigma surrounding Sharia Law. There is nothing unusual about a Semitic Middle Eastern religion having its own legal system. Judaism has one too. In fact, much of Islam's Sharia Law is actually based on Judaism's Halachic law. The anxiety in the West about Sharia Law is understandable because of people like Anjem Choudary in the UK and various other Imams that have called for Sharia courts to be established in the West.[41]

To start with, Sharia is not exactly what people in the West often think it is. It is not radically different from Jewish Halachic law. It's not really there to impose itself on the rest of the world through brute force. Rather it exists to provide Muslims meaning and order in their own lives.[42]

The traditional view, taught to most Muslims in their homes, is that Sharia is only applicable within Islamic lands. It cannot simply be forced on to non-Muslim lands the way that critics of Islam often assume it is. The issue is way more complex than that.

Many scholars believe that Sharia can only be implemented if most of the population wants it to. Sharia is for Muslims within Muslim lands. It doesn't even apply to the non-Muslims living within Muslim lands, let alone applying to non-Muslims in non-Muslim lands. The Ottoman Empire, for instance, had ecclesiastical courts to judge disputes between Jews, who were not subjected to Sharia Law. The Office of the Hakham Bashi is a perfect example of Jewish legal autonomy under the Ottoman Empire.[43]

Similarly, tolerant examples of Sharia not imposing itself upon ethnic and religious minorities also exist in the case of the Indian Subcontinent where the Mughals were the ruling class for over three centuries.

Many other aspects of Sharia law are often poorly understood. Private sins are usually dealt with through a private repentance. It is only public sins that necessitate public punishment. This is like Catholic adherents making confession at a Church. The difference is: there is no third-party intercession required in Islam. So instead of atoning for your sins through a Priest, a Muslim can talk directly to God anywhere, any time.

Sins are to be kept private. This is because Islam understands the imperfections inherent within human nature. Sharia understands that openly discussing what one does in private can encourage others to do the same, which risks the moral integrity of the society. This is something Islam takes seriously.

Authentic Sharia has therefore made it a sin for a Muslim to publicise another's private sins. This works out best for the individual and for society. Another big point to note is that for most Muslims, the word Sharia simply only means their personal relationship with God. So, things like praying five times a day, or fasting during Ramadan and being kind to everyone in general are all forms of abiding by the Sharia.

It is true that the other aspect of Sharia has a civic and legal component. That, as we have just learnt, only applies within Islamic territories. While Islam does aspire to spread itself to all corners of the earth, it does not prescribe aggressive military expansionism in order to achieve this. If anything, it discourages the forced imposition of Sharia onto non-Muslims.

The earliest political conquests that the Umayyads and the Abbasids experienced shortly after the death of Prophet Muhammad were, often, in response to aggression and acts of military hostility carried out by rivalling civilisations. It was extremely rare for the early Muslims to be the first to strike. For the most part, what is ideal for Muslims in our own times is to share Islam with the world through intelligent, civilised and respectful dialogue. This concept is called making *da'wah* in Islam, which literally means to invite someone to Islam. This method is preferred over expansion through warfare. If Muslims were under attack and had no choice but to retaliate, then just war out of self-defence is permissible in Islam.

Most important of all, as discussed earlier, in authentic Sharia courts, there is no trial until the evidentiary requirements of four adult male witnesses has been confirmed. One can imagine how impossibly rare it must be for four adult males to catch other people in the act. Unless those criteria are met, no prosecution may proceed. I hope this section clarifies any misconceptions. There is more on this topic in the next section. So how do people get their hands chopped off or stoned to death?

Caliphate: Does Islam require a theocratic state?

As discussed in previous sections, because Islam has its own set of laws, it requires some territory in order to form a jurisdiction. This form of a state may not be the horrible states attempted by Al-Qaeda, the Taliban and ISIS, but more peaceful versions of a Sunni

Muslim state – with leaders elected by scholars who know what Islam truly is – can be formed. These types of states certainly have functioned quite well in the past.

What a lot of people in the West fear about Islam is that there's an attempt being made to shove it down our throats. Instead of establishing a caliphate somewhere in the Muslim world, people in the West fear that attempts are being made to establish caliphates throughout Europe and the colonised West.

This is true of the certain areas of the United Kingdom where breakaway Muslims have tried to declare Sharia only zones.[44] This practice is strictly not in accordance with authentic Islam. The overwhelming majority of consensus within mainstream Islamic jurisprudence says, where there is no Islamic government, there is a duty on Muslims to live by the law of the land they are in.

The only exception is that if the law of the non-Muslim land where the Muslim might be living gets so tough to follow that the Muslim is no longer able to even privately practice his or her religion. Then the Muslim is obliged by religious jurisprudence to make *hijrah* that is, to migrate to another land where he or she can freely practice their faith. At no stage does it say that the Muslim should remain in the non-Muslim land where his practice of Islam is compromised by the law and end up rebelling against that system.

When in foreign lands, instead of being politically active to create some sort of a religious theocracy, Muslims are simply instructed to focus more on the personal and spiritual aspects of Islamic law. These include following the five pillars of Islam, which we've looked at previously. Even the notion of *jihad*, which critics of Islam understand to be 'holy war', in fact only means some sort of a struggle against one's self to strive to be the best person one can be.[46] It is synonymous with saying self-control.

Jihad does have another sense. Often understood to be the 6th invisible pillar of Islam, Jihad in the other sense means struggling against your opponent out of self-defence. Jihad is not supposed to be about aggressive warfare, imperialism or territorial acquisition by conquest, unless if the Muslim state was attacked first and it was about the protection of civilian lives. This is exactly like Christianity's concept of 'just war'.[47]

An Islamic theocratic state may function democratically in certain aspects if it is the will of the people, that's generally how things used to be in the past. There was never a single caliphate stretching across the connected landmass of the Islamic world from Morocco in the west to Pakistan in the east. There were multiple caliphates in different timeframes. To name a few, the Umayyads, Abbasids, Fatimids, Almohads, Ottomans, Mughals and Safavids are all classic examples of Muslim regimes across various stages of the last 14 centuries that have tended to refer to themselves as a caliphate. If a caliphate lives up to its authentic role and function in the life of a Muslim, and does not impose itself on the world outside of the Islam's traditional heartlands in North Africa and the Middle East, then such a theocratic state would essentially be exactly like the Vatican City and it would not bother the critics of Islam.

The problem with the way Al-Qaeda and ISIS have tried to position their violent bid for a caliphate is by terrorising the world using guerrilla warfare tactics and disregarding the proper rules of war as laid down by the Prophet of Islam and his immediate successors. The first Caliph of Islam, Abu Bakr Siddiq, who took charge of first caliphate after Prophet Muhammad, would say the following before launching defensive wars,

"You will find people who have devoted themselves to monasteries, leave them to their devotions... do not kill the old and feeble, women or children; do not destroy buildings; do not cut down trees or harm livestock; do not burn or drown palms; do not be treacherous; do not mutilate; do not be cowardly; and do not loot."[48]

This powerful quote was among the earliest things my mum taught me as a child. I would go so far as to say that most normal Muslims are taught the same. Once we start to understand this, we realise how average Muslims aren't raised any differently from the average-anyone-else. Whatever violence may or may not be otherwise mandated in certain religious teaching, it is safe to say most sensible people currently interpret things in a manner relevant to our times. That was the Islam that I grew up with. The most interesting point here is that the quote from Abu Bakr Siddiq above isn't even a secret. It is a mainstream quote that is well known by established scholars of Islam. The trouble is that 20th century jihadist movements with their own anti-US anti-Zionism attitudes have often gone back and made traditional Islam more extreme than it's meant to be. Suffice to say: the kind of caliphate Islam mandates is not the caliphate global terrorist organisations want to create. These are two different and competing objectives. We must never allow the extremists to hijack what Islam truly means.

Does the Quran preach hate?

Given the rise of terrorism, which has been a central theme of various sections of this book, many critics have naturally come to the most obvious conclusion they could come to. That is, if there is so much violence and bloodshed happening in the name of this religion, where crazy fanatics cry out "Allahu Akbar" before murdering innocents, then it must be that their religious scripture is full of hate. This on the surface is a completely logical and natural assumption to make.

The only problem with it is that it is oversimplified. Religious scripture, particularly in the Abrahamic faiths of Judaism, Christianity and Islam does not function the way many people think it does. You do not simply grab a random excerpt out of a text and take it literally as if it applies across all timeframes and in every situation. Most of the text contained within the Jewish Tanakh (Old Testament), the Christian New Testament or the

Islamic Quran requires context, commentaries, exegeses, scholarly opinions, and interpretation.

To use a familiar example, when we read the statement "If you drink and drive, you are a bloody idiot" in Australia, we all know that this statement is referring to an *alcoholic* drink. There is no doubt in the mind of an Aussie that this statement is surely not referring to tea, or coffee, or coca cola. Yet, notice that statement itself does not actually refer to which type of a drink. It simply says, "if you drink and drive". We know that it means alcohol because, as Australians, we know the context.

The same is true when trying to make sense of religious scripture. To turn our focus to the Jewish Tanakh or Old Testament, there is whole section of the book of Deuteronomy where God tells Joshua how to go to war against different ethnic groups and to execute them and take their belongings. Chapter 20 of this book mentions by name the ethnic groups that are supposed to be killed. Joshua is told by God to destroy the Hittites, Amorites, Canaanites, Perizzites, Hivites and Jebusites.

This exact passage reads more violently than anything remotely comparable to the Quran. Refer below:

> 20 When you go to war against your enemies and see horses and chariots and an army greater than yours, do not be afraid of them, because the Lord your God, who brought you up out of Egypt, will be with you. 2 When you are about to go into battle, the priest shall come forward and address the army. 3 He shall say: "Hear, Israel: Today you are going into battle against your enemies. Do not be faint hearted or afraid; do not panic or be terrified by them. 4 For the Lord your God is the one who goes with you to fight for you against your enemies to give you victory."
>
> 5 The officers shall say to the army: "Has anyone built a new house and not yet begun to live in it? Let him go home, or he

may die in battle and someone else may begin to live in it. **6** Has anyone planted a vineyard and not begun to enjoy it? Let him go home, or he may die in battle and someone else enjoy it. **7** Has anyone become pledged to a woman and not married her? Let him go home, or he may die in battle and someone else marry her."

8 Then the officers shall add, "Is anyone afraid or fainthearted? Let him go home so that his fellow soldiers will not become disheartened too." **9** When the officers have finished speaking to the army, they shall appoint commanders over it.

10 When you march up to attack a city, make its people an offer of peace. **11** If they accept and open their gates, all the people in it shall be subject to forced labor and shall work for you. **12** If they refuse to make peace and they engage you in battle, lay siege to that city. **13** When the Lord your God delivers it into your hand, put to the sword all the men in it. **14** As for the women, the children, the livestock and everything else in the city, you may take these as plunder for yourselves. And you may use the plunder the Lord your God gives you from your enemies. **15** This is how you are to treat all the cities that are at a distance from you and do not belong to the nations nearby.

16 However, in the cities of the nations the Lord your God is giving you as an inheritance, do not leave alive anything that breathes. **17** Completely destroy them — the Hittites, Amorites, Canaanites, Perizzites, Hivites and Jebusites — as the Lord your God has commanded you. **18** Otherwise, they will teach you to follow all the detestable things they do in worshiping their gods, and you will sin against the Lord your God.

19 When you lay siege to a city for a long time, fight against it to capture it, do not destroy its trees by putting an ax to them, because you can eat their fruit. Do not cut them down. Are the trees people, that you should besiege them? **20** However, you may cut down trees that you know are not fruit trees and use them to build siege works until the city at war with you falls.[49]

Most people who believe in the Bible do not even know that these verses exist. Yet this verse remains a real eye opener for those who claim that the existence of violent mandate within a religious text means that the followers of that religion will turn out violent. It doesn't always follow.

There were Jewish paramilitary groups during the British mandate of Palestine from 1920 to 1948 and Stern, Lehi, Irgun and the Haganah are classic examples of that.[50] These days, there are no Jewish terrorist groups at all.

This point alone clarifies many things. In the first instance, it compels us to understand that just because a book contains a few violent passages, that doesn't mean that its adherents will necessarily turn out violent or hateful. In the second instance, the fact that Jewish paramilitary groups only existed during the independence struggles for Israel but ceased to exist afterwards suggests that asymmetric warfare or terrorism is practically always motivated by political goals.

Hence, quoting from that Chapter 20 in Deuteronomy and citing the genocide of those Hittites, Amorites, Canaanites, Perizzites, Hivites and Jebusites as an attempt to prove that Judaism is a violent religion does not work. Judaism is not a violent religion and the Jews are not a violent people even though this Chapter 20 clearly contains the mandate for religious and political violence.

This is because most Jews do not read that verse out of context. They know that this particular verse is a product of an ancient time and it does not apply perpetually across all ages. It was a specific instruction given to Joshua for a specific timeframe and the validity of that violent mandate is well past its expiry date.

The same is true of the Quran. Many Quranic verses were revealed during times of war. Remember, as mentioned earlier, the political turmoil that was rampant in Arabia during the Prophet Muhammad's times? His own Quraish tribe was hell-bent on persecuting early

Muslims because they were seen as a threat by most of Prophet Muhammad's own uncles who were part of the ruling elite. The Prophet did what he could to maintain peace between Muslims and non-Muslims with whatever limited capacity he had.

He signed peace treaties wherever he could and with whoever was willing. The Constitution of Madinah which we have also spoken about in other sections is a classic example. The Treaty of Hudaibiyah is yet another example of the Prophet's diplomacy and tendency to settle for peace where he could. But those were hostile times. On too many occasions, the other party failed to keep its end of the bargain and war became a last resort.

Many wars were fought during the 23 years of Muhammad's life since becoming a Prophet at age 40. The Battles of Badr, Uhud and Tabuk are notable examples. Muslims were usually not the first to start the war; they were drawn into conflict in retaliation. It was within this context many of those verses of the Quran often cited by the critics of Islam as mandating violence come into the picture.

For instance, where the Quran says in Surah Al-Baqarah at verse 191: "Slay the unbelievers wherever you find them." this is not an instruction by God to the entire human race across all ages and timeframes. This is a specific order to be followed during those times of political turmoil when Muslims were under attack by the ruling Quraish tribe. It is the same as Deuteronomy Chapter 20.

It was within the same context that the Quran in Surah Al-Imran at verse 28 says, "Muslims must not take the infidels as friends". There are hundreds of other verses of the same nature throughout the Quran just as there are hundreds of other equally violent passages throughout the Old Testament. We don't need to cite them all here because by this stage, I'm sure you already get the point. Nothing can be understood without context.

The conclusion is that Islam is neither a religion of war nor a religion of peace. It is a realistic religion with a practical approach to life. When you are under attack, you are permitted to fight back. This is the same as what any modern nation-state does. Why does Australia have 30 thousand active full-time soldiers in our defence force? This doesn't mean we're a violent country or that our Constitution preaches hate. It simply means we have a right to defend our people.

Islam is realistic enough to give Muslims the same right to self-defence. When a religion doesn't give its followers that right to defend themselves, they create that right manually. This happened in the case of Christianity which says to "love your enemy" and "to turn the other cheek", two often quoted teachings of Jesus found in the New Testament. These ideals sound great in theory but they cannot be adopted as a nation's foreign policy.

Imagine your enemy is at the door wanting to invade your country, usurp its resources and enslave your people. Are you going to turn around and start loving the enemy and turning the other cheek? By the time you are done spreading your love, you won't have a country left. It's completely understandable that when Christianity was adopted as the Roman Empire's state religion in 381 AD, Church Fathers had to create a mandate for warfare as a means for self-defence. St Augustine and St Thomas Aquinas' 'just war' theory is exactly that adaptation.

In Judaism and Islam, those rights to defend one's self do not need to be invented by Saints because they're mandated within the core scripture itself. It is important not to perceive these mandates as proof of hatred, or of imperialism, or terrorism, but rather as proof of a right to self-defence. Cherry-picking a few random lines out of the Quran and ignoring centuries of tafseer (exegeses) that explains its meanings with context cannot be ignored. So, in short, the answer is no, the Quran does not preach hate nor violence. To the contrary, it preaches justice, love and compassion as its core message.

Was Prophet Muhammad violent towards Jews and Christians?

When Islam began as a movement, it was met with fierce resistance by its founder's own tribe, the Quraish, who were pagans based in Mecca. Early Muslims migrated and sought refuge in neighbouring town Madinah, which was itself torn apart by tribal warfare between the Banu Aws and Banu Khazraj tribes.

Prophet Muhammad issued a document called Methaq Al-Madinah or the Charter of Madinah in 622 CE, one of the earliest peace treaties in the world, which constituted peace between early Muslims, Jews, Pagans and Christians. It referred to them all as *Ummah Wahida* or One Nation. Madinah began to flourish as a tolerant, pluralistic multi-religious society.

As per the terms of this treaty, religious freedoms were protected. There were rules laid down prohibiting warfare except in self-defence, and there was a complex judicial system for resolving tribal disputes. No weapons were to be carried and no blood to be spilt unless in a state of war.

On one occasion, an argument broke out between a Jewish man and a Muslim woman. He stripped her naked publicly, a Muslim man killed the Jew. Some Jews in turn killed a bunch of Muslims out of revenge; factions within each side launched a spree of revenge killings and growing enmity then led to the Prophet Muhammad seeking to exterminate the entire Jewish tribe of Banu Qaynuqa. This was not because they were "Jewish" but because their key member had violated the Charter of Madinah (622), yet at the pleas of their chief Rabbi he settled for expelling them instead.

Similarly, the Jewish tribe of Banu Nadir was expelled for plotting the assassination of the Prophet Muhammad. The Jewish tribe of Banu Qurayza was exterminated because it first sided with the early Muslims in battle against the Quraish, later betrayed them during war. As a result, all the men, the fighting force, of Banu Qurayza were executed, while their women and children were sold as slaves, not because they were "Jewish" but due to their deflection to the other side in an on-going military conflict.

It must be borne in mind, that the United States among other Western nations to date continues to practice capital punishment for military sedition against the interests of the State. There were many Jewish families and individuals who continued to live peacefully alongside early Muslims despite the expulsion of the Banu Qaynuqa and Banu Nadir, and despite the extermination of the Banu Qurayza.

The Prophet Muhammad had good relations with Jewish neighbours, and often visited them when they were sick. If the early Muslims were such savages seeking to exterminate every Jew because he was a Jew, how then did the Sephardic and Mizrahi Jews survive as a successful and thriving community in Yemen, Iraq and other parts of the Arabian Peninsula?

People's assessment of the treatment of early Muslims at the hands of Jews is exactly like those left-wing arguments in our own nation, seeking to put forward the view that there were massacres upon massacres of Indigenous Australians by European settlers. By so doing, critics are running an identical and equally flawed line of reasoning, making broadly generalised claims devoid of historical context. To draw an Australian parallel, native Indigenous Australians often attacked European farmers and their cattle, which would then lead to retaliation.

The Myall Creek incident, which has since been dubbed the Myall Creek "massacre" is a case in point. Thirty Indigenous people were killed by ten Europeans in 1838 in Bingara, New South Wales, not because these natives were "Indigenous" but because they had attacked farmers and cattle in the first instance. Remember, context is always important.

The relationship between Jews and Muslims, for the most part, has been surprisingly harmonious and cordial.

Of course, that relationship has deteriorated in recent times, but this is largely due to the on-going Israeli-Palestinian conflict. In actual fact, Islam is based on Judaism. All the Jewish prophets from Adam himself the first human, right through to the prophets mentioned in the Old Testament, all of these figureheads are revered and respected within Islamic thought.

The theological similarities between Judaism and Islam by far outweigh both their collective similarities with Christianity that has a 'triune' concept of God; that is God the father, God the son and God the Holy Spirit. Christians insist this is not a form of paganism or polytheism, but in both Jewish and Islamic thought God is supposed to be 'indivisible'. So, suggesting God has three distinct forms, as father, son and Holy Spirit at the same time violates this notion.

In fact, the very first commandment to the ancient Israelites was "Thou Shalt Have No other Gods Besides Me". When Jews pray, they remind themselves of what is called the Shema, which is a statement of belief that says: Shema Yisrael, Adonai Eloheinu, Adonai Echad. This means "Hear O Israel, The Lord your God, is One God".[51] This is comparable to the Quranic verse: Qul hu Allahu ahad, Allahus Samad, Lam Yalid, wa lam Yulad, walam yaku l-lahu kufu an ahad. This means, "Say your God is One God, He is the Absolute, He does not beget, nor is he begotten and there is no one else like Him".[52]

This rule's out any concept of the Christian Trinity being welcome in Judeo-Islamic scholarly thought. Due to this theological synergy between the two faiths, they were traditional allies and historically, the Christian Crusaders were the enemy. When the Crusaders marched into Jerusalem in 1095, they massacred 70,000 women, men and children in a single day. This included both Jews and Muslims.

The Jews fought alongside Muslims to repel the Christians during the Crusades. The Battle of Hattin is a classic example, where the victorious Muslim army was aided by some Jewish cavalry. It's therefore important that we do not look at the historical dynamic between Jews and Muslims through the prism of the Israeli-Palestinian conflict. For the most part of their history, Jews have tended to not only get along better with Muslims; they thrived as a community within the Islamic world.

There are many historical examples of this Judeo-Islamic synergy that would stand to challenge our contemporary views on the broken dynamic between the two people since the start of the Zionist movement. Take for example the fact that almost 13 centuries ago when Spanish Jews were sick of institutionalised antisemitism under Christian Visigothic King Roderick II, they rejoiced in the Muslim army of Tariq Bin Ziyad's takeover of Spain. What followed was the Jewish Golden Age of learning and literature. This is the age that produced Judaism's greatest ever scholar by the name of Moshe Ben Maimon who is also known in English as Moses Maimonides, or simply 'Rambam'.

There are more examples. The renowned Jewish scholar Hasdai Ben Shaprut flourished in the Cordoban court of Caliph Abdul Rahman III. Jewish traveller Benyamin Mi-Tudela glorifies the Caliph Al-Mustadi's peaceful and tolerant rule in Baghdad in his book *Sefer Ha-Masaot*. Writing in the 12th century, the Jewish chronicler described the Muslim Caliph as follows:

> "He is truthful and trusty, speaking peace to all men... He is a benevolent man. He built, on the other side of the river, on the banks of an arm of the Euphrates which there borders the city, a hospital consisting of blocks of houses and hospices for the sick poor to come to be healed. Here there are about 60 physicians' stores which are provided from the Caliph's house with medicines and whatever else may be required. Every sick man who comes is maintained at the Caliph's expense and is

medically treated. In Baghdad there are about 40,000 Jews, and they dwell in security, prosperity and honour under the great Caliph, and amongst them are great sages, the heads of the Academies engaged in the study of the law."[53]

This is a well-known quote among learned Muslims and Jews. Sadly, very few Westerners know about it. Jewish civilisation's greatest scholar Rabbi Moses Maimonides who we mentioned earlier was a physician and an adviser to Sultan Saladin. This is the great Saladin who fought the Christian king Richard the Lionheart in the Crusades. When the Spanish Inquisition happened in 1492 it was Ottoman Sultan Bayezid II who sent the Ottoman Royal Navy to bring the expelled Jews safely into the Ottoman Empire and resettle them. This is where we get today's Sephardic and Mizrahi Jews from.

The point about Visigothic Spain, the quote from Binyamin Mi-Tudela, and the facts on Moses Maimonides and Sultan Bayezid II are the pillars of evidence upon which my contention stands in saying that Jews and Muslims have historically not been enemies and rivals. I can still recall how mum always used to say if you learn Islamic history, you'd have a much more positive take on Islam than the media presents today.

Having grown up, I see what mum meant. I could think of no better way of bringing this section to an end than to share this beautiful little-known passage from the Prophet Muhammad's pledge of peace towards the Christians in Mount Sinai:

> "This is a message from Muhammad ibn Abdullah, as a covenant to those who adopt Christianity – near and far, we are with them. Verily I, the servants, the helpers and my followers defend because Christians are my citizens: and by God I hold out against anything that displeases them. No compulsion is to be on them. Neither are their judges to be removed from their jobs nor their monks from their monasteries. No one is

to destroy a house of their religion, to damage it, or to carry anything from it to the Muslims' houses. Should anyone take any of these, he would spoil God's covenant and disobey His prophet. Verily, they are my allies and have my secure charter against all that they hate. No one is to force them to travel or oblige them to fight. The Muslims are to fight for them. If a female Christian is married to a Muslim, it is not to take place without her approval. She is not to be prevented from visiting her church to pray. Their churches are declared to be protected. They are neither to be prevented from repairing them nor the sacredness of their covenants. No one of the nation (Muslims) is to disobey the covenant until the last day (end of the world)."[54]

4
MYTHS AND FACTS II ISLAMIC SOCIAL PRACTICES

In the last section we busted some common myths about Islam's political side. In this section we will do the same with Islam's social practices. There are few religions on this planet that have attracted greater rebuke and global condemnation for their actual and imaginary strange practices, than Islam. I am not agreeing that Islam necessarily has any strange practices, but I certainly acknowledge that its critics think that it does.

For too long these misconceptions haven't been confronted head on because qualified Muslims that have the knowledge to do so are too often so emotional that they end up labelling their critics 'Islamophobic' rather than to actually bother addressing their concerns.

Often, critics of Islam don't make negative conclusions about Islam following independent research or critical thinking. By contrast, it's usually because they've managed to get their hands on some grudgeful book written by an ex-Muslim and decided to take its word for granted. My impression of their reasoning goes something like this: 'I read book x, written by an ex-Muslim who went through hell, therefore this person knows what they're talking about, and since I don't have the expertise to challenge what they're saying, I'll just run with its conclusions'.

Ask yourself: does being an Australian critic of Australia automatically validate every one of your criticisms? No. There are plenty of Australians in the Greens party who think that this country is built on stolen land and we are responsible for paying reparations to Indigenous Australians.[55] Most sensible Australians disagree with this, but just because those who put forward these ideas happen to be Australians themselves, does that mean they are experts on all things Australian? Of course not.

The same courtesy should apply to Islam. When a person quits Islam, often it isn't due to intellectual deficiencies within Islam. If you dig a little deeper, usually you'll find they have a problem with Muslims, as in the people, or the community and they end up taking out their anger and frustration on the religion itself. In some cases, the person departing Islam does do so for intellectual reasons, but having met, known and spoken to countless ex-Muslims, I would say this is rare.

As you saw in the first chapter of this book, my promise was to take you on a journey that would challenge your misconceptions considering my own upbringing and life experiences as a Muslim. Obviously, we have all heard that Muslims engage in all that horrible stuff such as honour killings, female genital mutilation and apparently, they lie and kill their apostates. Brace yourself: you're about to go on a ride that takes you to the truth.

Muslim Women: Are they really equal?

The status of women in Islam has been a highly contentious issue for Western observers of Islam. In a certain encounter in recent years between a Muslim activist and an Australian Senator on an episode of ABC's Q&A, it was claimed that Islam was the most feminist religion in the world.[56] This point is neither right nor wrong. It is simply a random, nonsensical statement uttered without any context whatsoever.

The crucial topic of conversation about the rights and role of women in Islam should have featured the historical backdrop against which Islam came into existence. In the 7th century Arabia, prior to the advent of Islam, women were treated terribly by pagan Arabs. It was a highly misogynistic and male dominated patriarchal society. In fact, it wasn't just Arabia, the entire world used to be like that. Neither the ancient Greeks, Vikings, Romans, Chinese nor Indians were any different. We often seem to forget that all those great philosophers of ancient Greece such as Socrates, Plato and Aristotle were all men. Even their greatest ever warriors such as Pericles and Alexander the Great were men. Were there no women in ancient Greece?

The only famous women we can think of from that age is Helen of Troy and to her detriment, even she is portrayed as having betrayed her husband for another lover. The same happens in the Roman Empire. From Julius Caesar to Marcus Aurelius, every notable Roman mentioned in history was male. Except again, the case of Cleopatra who, much like Helen of Troy is portrayed as a harlot. From these examples, we can clearly see what the world was like in ancient times. Women are either left out of history or only remembered as sexually corrupt. The Arabs in the 7th century were so fond of the idea that your first-born child ought to be a son that they used to habitually bury their first-born daughters alive until they had a son. The only way an Arab family could have an actual daughter was if they'd had a son first. A daughter could be a second or third born, but not first-born.

Women in those days were unable to run and operate businesses. Prophet Muhammad's wife Khadija, whom he married at age 25 when she was 40 in the days before he declared his prophethood, was a wealthy merchant but her case is the exception, rather than the rule in Arabia. The Arabs were fond of drinking, gambling, betting and prostitution.

After the Prophet Muhammad declared his prophethood, he immediately put an end to these malpractices prevalent within Arabia at the time. One of the earliest reforms was to outlaw the practice of burying daughters alive. He legislated for women to be able to run and operate businesses freely. He also decreed that women could retain their maiden names after marrying.

He encouraged women to become educated and play a critical role in the civic affairs of the society in which they lived. Whilst he taught that a woman's role in society is primarily centered on the household and child-rearing (which conservative Jews and Christians would agree with) the Prophet of Islam allowed women to join him on the battlefield in key positions when defending Muslims in the face of persecution. Women prior to Islam were unable to initiate a divorce; the Prophet of Islam changed this and allowed women to be able to initiate divorces.

For example, Nusaybah Bint Ka'ab also known as Umm Ammarah was one of the earliest female disciples of the Prophet.[57] She was a warrior who took part in the Battle of Uhud. She was known for her skilfulness with the sword and astonished those who saw her. She defended the Prophet in all directions.[58]

What happened in that infamous episode of ABC's Q&A where it was claimed by the Muslim activist that Islam was the most feminist religion in the world was an absolute farce. No doubt, as you can see, this is a sophisticated topic that requires greater nuances to delve into, as we have done so far in this section. People on that panel in that episode neither had the expertise nor the time to delve into these nuances.

If the Muslim activist had made the argument I have made in this section, and pointed out the kind of male dominated world the ancient world used to be, and then proceeded to arguing that relative to the norms of those times, Islam did uplift the status of women by a million degrees, nobody could have disagreed with her.

We hear about the suffering of Muslim women, such as Malala Yousafzai, but a closer examination of the realities within the Islamic world, paints a very different picture – one that's often left out of the conversation in mainstream media in the Western world. Who are we to be assuming how most Muslim women think? Let them speak for themselves. There's no shortage of successful Muslim women who do not feel oppressed. Neither do they feel unequal to men.

Scholars note that, "Muslim women gained rights unparalleled in the world. In fact, Muslim women enjoyed more rights than women in any other society until the liberation of women in the Western world".[59] This claim is not dissimilar from what was said on Q&A and now that you know the historical context of the 7th century you can appreciate why so many Muslims believe Islam to be a feminist religion.

By the time Islamic law began to be codified in the 8th century CE various pre-Islamic practices and non-Islamic influences such as Hellenistic and Sassanid cultures had affected the dominant thinking.[60] This often meant that through foreign cultural influences becoming submerged with Islamic culture, women went from being treated exceptionally well to being relegated to a subordinate status. Still, this was the exception rather than the rule.

For the most part, Islam itself has treated women as equals with men. The exact roles of men and women in society are, however, different. There has been a diversity of thought among scholars on their respective roles within society. Fatima Mernissi of Morocco takes a more liberal stance on the matter while Abbas Mahmud Al-Aqqad takes a more conservative view.[61] The Prophet's wife Aisha was the commander of her army and she excelled in the highest form of etiquette as a prominent role model for other Muslim women.

It surprises many to learn that not only is the Al-Qarawiyyin University the world's oldest continuing degree offering academic institution, more interestingly it was established by a woman by the name of Fatima Al-Fihri in the Moroccan city of Fez in the year 859.[62] Equally interesting is that most countries have a founding father, Pakistan on the other hand had the towering personality of Fatima Jinnah, who became the founding mother of Pakistan. In that country she is known as Madr-e-Millat, which in English translates as the "Mother of the Nation".[63]

Former Pakistani Prime Minister Benazir Bhutto notes in her autobiography that "Islam in fact had been quite progressive towards women from its inception: the Prophet Muhammad had forbidden the killing of female infants common among the Arabs of the time, and called for education for women and their right to inherit long before these privileges were granted to them in the West".[64]

She goes on to note that, "Muslim history was full of women who had taken a public role and performed every bit as successfully as men. Nothing in Islam discouraged them, or me, from pursuing that course."[65] Benazir Bhutto points out that Chand Bibi the female ruler of the Indian state of Ahmadnagar defeated the Mughal Emperor Akbar forcing him to enter into a peace treaty with her. The Mughal Emperor Jehangir's wife Noor Jehan is another example of a skilful female ruler in Mughal India.

These success stories about Muslim women and the prominent roles they played throughout history are an important part of the wider debate on Islam and women. It is all too tempting for people, especially in the West, to look at Islam and jump to the conclusion it treats women as second-class citizens. We must consider both sides of the argument.

There is no use jumping on a random website that makes all sorts of claims to make Islam appear oppressive, sexist and misogynistic then go off and agree with everything it says. Remember, that could also be done with Judaism and Christianity. Plenty of critics think they know what the Talmud is all about when they have never even met or spoken to a single Jew nor heard his perspective. Plenty of critics think they know Christianity or Christian history when they have never even met or spoken to a single Christian nor heard their perspective. There's plenty of antisemitic material available on the Internet that says the most vile and horrible things about Jews. Do we need to use that content to decide how we should think about Jews or their religion? Absolutely not.

Perhaps the most vital point I should make is that I don't know these stories because I'm particularly well read. I know these stories because I learnt them and internalised them growing up in a Muslim household. Whatever culture or religious tradition you identify with, ask yourself, did your mother not sing you lullabies, or teach you stories when you were little? Did you not internalise the narratives at home that used to come up in conversation with parents? Of course, you did, everyone does that. And those narratives *are* you; they are what your community *actually* believes.

No part of a Jew's upbringing involves his or her parents telling him about world domination. Yet that is the thing anti-Semites always accuse Jews of. Now if you had plenty of Jewish friends, you'd know for yourself these people are as normal as anyone else. They want to wake up, go to work, come home, put food on the table, put kids to sleep, retire, go on a holiday, give their children better lives than they had. Isn't that what everyone wants? So, where's the global domination in any of that?

Why do anti-Semites continue to hold those beliefs about Jews? It's all too easy to judge a whole community and make up all sorts of perceptions about them and their alleged weirdness inside our minds. Anyone can do that if we have conversations with ourselves. So, don't. Go and have that conversation with an actual person who knows their stuff as an insider. Listen to what their parents raised them to believe. That's the most important part of the process of understanding somebody else.

Rather than thinking you have the authority to speak on behalf of a Muslim woman, let the woman speak for herself. Public opinions are always split down the middle, that's the nature of public opinions. You'll get the Iranian woman who hates wearing the Hijab just as you'll get the Iranian woman who loves wearing the Hijab. The one who hates it will say she was forced to wear it. The one who loves it will say she chose to put it on.

Either way, who are we to tell them what they should and shouldn't wear? Especially if they're doing it in their own countries. I'm all for banning the Burqa as a fundamental axiom of Australian society, we want to see your face in public, but Burqa is not the same as Hijab. Besides, why should we pick one Iranian woman's view and make it out to be representative of most? We must know when not to judge. We always sound egotistical on the issue of feminism. I'd go so far as to say that those of us on the right often do it with a degree of hypocrisy. Let me explain. Conservatives on the right of politics will gladly tell you that feminism has ruined our society; it started off as a noble movement but now it's lost the plot, gone beyond the intent of its founders, is now about hating men. Maybe some of that's true. But in the same breath, those conservatives will gladly side with the radical feminists in Iran and Saudi Arabia.

So if a bunch of nude feminist women were to storm a university theatre in Sydney, New York or London, the conservatives in the West will say they are shameful and have no respect for maintaining decency in public. But if nude feminist women did the same in Riyadh or Tehran? Believe me: that same conservative will side with the radical feminist and not the society's establishment. Why the double standards? Because it's always easier to judge others. But as Jesus Christ famously said, "judge not, lest ye be judged". Sometimes, it is important to remember that. That attitude is the cornerstone of the Christian foundations of our morality.

So many of our critics in other parts of the world look at us Westerners and judge us in ways we don't even realise. But they're only doing to us, what we do to them. For instance, in Latin America, Asia and Africa, the question is often asked, 'why has America never had a female President?' The first American Presidential election was held in 1789 when George Washington was sworn in as the inaugural office holder.

It has been 230 years. That's right, two hundred and thirty years (at the time of writing this book in 2019!) and the world's greatest superpower, the bastion of freedom and democracy, with a current population of 330 million, still hasn't managed to find a single woman for the top job? How does that work? Why doesn't this ever come up in conversation among us? Why are we obsessed with talking about the alleged gender inequality in other societies? America had the opportunity to vote for a woman in 2016. It didn't - and I'm glad it didn't because she wasn't a good choice. That however still doesn't excuse the fact that in more than 230 years, they still haven't been able to find one. The most populous Muslim nation in the world, Indonesia, has in fact had a female President from 2001 to 2004 in Megawati Sukarnoputri, the first female to take that office.[66]

Similarly, Tansu Ciller became the first female Prime Minister of Turkey in 1993. Her ascent into Turkish politics encouraged many other women to follow in her footsteps and enter politics.[67] In Bangladesh, there has been a case where both the sitting Prime Minister Begum Khaleda Zia and her Opposition Leader Sheikh Hasina were both females at the same time from 2001 to 2006.[68] Zia was in fact ranked by the Forbes Magazine in 2005 as the 29th most powerful woman in the world. She was responsible for the restoration of democracy after the nation's military phase. Further to these, the Muslim-majority nation of Kyrgyzstan in 2010 swore in an atheist woman, Roza Otunbayeva as a female President. Atifete Jahjaga became Kosovo's first female President at

36; the youngest head of state to ever be elected. She was previously a Deputy Director of the Kosovo Police and worked her way up to being a Major General before entering politics. She hosted an International Women's Summit in 2012 inviting 200 leaders from all over the world.[70]

Mama Madior Boye was Prime Minister of Senegal from 2001 to 2002. She was a real feminist who actually worked hard for the women of her country, not the third wave radical feminists we have in the West.[71] There has even been a case of a Muslim woman ruling a non-Muslim country; Ameenah Fakim was sworn in as the President of Mauritius in 2015.[72] Queen Rania of Jordan is another example of a female leader and prominent figure in the Muslim world.[73]

While most of our examples of successful Muslim women are fairly recent, it must be pointed out that liberating women and respecting them in roles of political authority is actually not a recent development in Islamic thought, as it is in Western thought. The mistake Western critics of Islam often make, is that they presume the evolution of Islamic societies has occurred on the same linear trajectory as their own society.

Around a century or so ago, women did not have the right to vote. It was not until the 19th Amendment to the American Constitution in 1920 that women were first able to participate in American democracy. So, for a country that declared its independence on 4th July 1776, we're talking about 144 years when women were relegated to the kitchen, where they cooked, cleaned, did the laundry and raised kids. For an entire century and a half, in a country as first world as America, women did not even have the right to vote. How about that?

During the 1800s by contrast, Queen Victoria of the British Empire had forged a deeply affectionate relationship with her Indian Muslim servant by the name of Abdul Karim. This theme has been the subject of the film Victoria & Abdul in 2017, which somewhat exaggeratedly portrays a basic fact that did occur over a century ago. Abdul Karim used to teach Victoria the Urdu language as well as about Islam. None of this could have been possible if Abdul Karim had been conditioned to think of women as his subordinates.[74] If the Islamic world or its values were as backward and sexist as the critics of Islam make it out to be, then the Islamic world would not be leading the charge in putting so many more female leaders on the world map than the Western world.

No society is perfect, and we certainly have our fair share of social problems in Australia. Anyone who followed the career of former Prime Minister Julia Gillard would know how marginalised she felt being the first female Prime Minister of this first world nation of ours.[75]

On almost a daily basis, Gillard was criticised for things she didn't deserve. People made fun of her hair colour, physique, accent and just about everything she did. She was attacked outside Parliament House with people throwing sandwiches and other items at her on one occasion.[76] Gillard's famous misogyny speech is an indication of the extent to which she felt that her gender was an issue for her in politics.

Another towering Australian woman politician, One Nation leader Pauline Hanson went to jail two decades ago. This did not mean that she went to jail because we hate women, it happened because there was a case against her. But mentioning this is important, because if the same kind of thing had happened to a Muslim woman leader in the Islamic world, chances are we would have presumed that the woman went to jail *because* she was a woman.

As a matter of fact, people already do pursue that way of thinking about the assassination of former Pakistani Prime Minister Benazir Bhutto. Critics think her murder is proof of how sexist and misogynistic the Islamic world is. This is absurd reasoning.

The United States has had four Presidents assassinated. These are Abraham Lincoln, William McKinley, James A. Garfield and John F. Kennedy. All males. Does this mean that Americans hate men? We know politics is a brutal game and people have enemies. If someone hates you, it is generally because you stand for something. Your enemies don't care about your gender; they care that you are a threat to them. And it is true, in our own case that Pauline Hanson was a threat to the mainstream conservative political parties because considerable numbers of voters were defecting to her.

As a proud Australian woman, I have never felt disadvantaged nor discriminated against in any shape or form. Truth be told, I have probably given men a much tougher time in my line of work than the other way around. Everybody is different and we all have our own unique experiences.

As a woman, and a Muslim one at that, I would not for the life of me try to downplay the way former Prime Minister Julia Gillard felt about her time in office as a woman. Those are her experiences and they ought to be understood on their own terms. If nothing else, her experiences stand as a proof that we as a society are far from perfect. There may not be any structural flaws within our culture as far as our treatment of women is concerned, but the mere fact someone out there could feel that way remains cause for concern, regardless. People who live in glasshouses shouldn't throw stones.

Forced conversions

Critics of Islam generally believe that Islam spread by the sword and large numbers of people were forcibly converted. On the contrary, the Quran actually says 'la ikraha fi-d deen' which means 'there is no compulsion in religion'.[77] Again, the trouble with many Western critics is they tend to interpret the course of Islamic history and the nature of Islamic practices through the prism of Christian history.

It is true that when Christianity spread across much of Europe,

Christian warrior kings like Charlemagne and William the Conqueror were brutal in their forced conversions of the people they conquered. William the Conqueror is well known for his slaughter of thousands upon thousands of Vikings and Saxons. There are no pre-Christian religions left alive in Europe anymore.

Before Christianity, Europe used to have the ancient Greek religion, the ancient Roman religion, the ancient Norse religion and the ancient Druid religion. These cultures have now become extinct precisely because people like Charlemagne and William the Conqueror wiped them out through their 'convert or die' policy. The only religion that was around in Europe alongside Christianity all this while was Judaism, and even the Jews faced incredible degrees of antisemitism, pogroms, mass expulsions and genocide.[78]

Remember, the Holocaust did not happen in the Middle East. The Jews of the Middle East lived in peace and harmony alongside Muslims, for the most part. Specific historical examples of the tolerance towards Jews are mentioned in the relevant section on the Prophet Muhammad's treatment of Jews. In the end, ask yourself why the State of Israel even had to be created in the first place. It was because Jews weren't safe in Europe. So 1948, after 2,000 years of Jewish persecution at the hands of Christian Europeans, at last a state was created on the world map so that Jews could rule over Jews in their own sovereign territory.

By contrast, wherever you look within the Islamic world, there are minority religions literally everywhere. In my own parents' country of origin, Lebanon, half the population is Maronite Christian.[79] There is even a deal between the ruling factions within Lebanon where the President is always a Maronite Christian, the Prime Minister is a Sunni Muslim and the Speaker of Parliament is always a Shi'ite Muslim.[80] Even we, here in Australia, don't have such arrangements within Australia where the Governor-General had to be, say, Indigenous and the Prime Minister non-Indigenous.

In Egypt, the city of Alexandria is home to the oldest continuing communities of Eastern Christianity, the Coptic branch.[81] In Syria, not only are there Christian communities of the Orthodox Syriac order, they are the world's only community of people who still speak Aramaic as a native tongue, which was the first language of Jesus Christ and his disciples.[82] In Bethlehem, in the Palestinian Territories, the birthplace of Jesus Christ, there was also the world's oldest Christian Palestinian communities who trace their ancestry back to the disciples of Jesus.

In Iran, there are thousands of Jews, with representation in Parliament.[83] Iran is also home to as many Christians of the Chalcedonian branch. The Jews of the Middle East are referred to as Sephardim and Mizrahim. They for the most part lived side by side in peace with Muslims for 14 centuries, with nothing remotely like the Holocaust ever happening anywhere in the Islamic world.[84] As renowned Jewish intellectual David J Wasserstein famously said: "Had Islam not come along, Jewry in the west would have declined to disappearance and Jewry in the east would have become just another oriental cult."[85]

In fact, the Ottoman Empire saved the Jews from persecution in Europe by offering them asylum in the city of Thessaloniki, which was part of the Ottoman Empire, which is now in the modern state of Greece.[86] The Ottoman Empire had special ecclesiastical courts to allow Jews legal autonomy within its own broader civic structures. The office of *Hakham Bashi* was the Rabbinate within the Ottoman Empire.[87] Jews lived with considerable degrees of autonomy under Islamic rule.

By today's standards, it's easy for critics to say, 'But the Jews were still subordinate to Muslims under Islamic rule'. My response to that would be: name one culture in the world where minorities have not been treated as subordinately? Should we start digging up everyone's histories? Ask the Scots how they were treated by the English. Ask the Catalans how they are still treated today by Spain.

Ask the Rohingyas how they are treated in Burma. The point is the dominant group treating its minorities as subordinates was not the exception throughout history. It was the rule. Even today it exists in a mixture of direct and indirect forms.

So, the question we should be asking is not, whether or not Islam treated its minorities as subordinates. The real question is: did Islam treat its minorities better or worse than other cultures in the same timeframes? Given the argument I have presented, you decide.

Ask yourself why no minority religions in Europe survive today and the one religion, Judaism, that did exist in Europe, was profoundly discriminated against by institutionalised Christianity. Ask yourself, why in the Islamic world, there are still Mizrahi Jews, Coptic, Maronite, Syriac and Chalcedonian Christian communities? If Islam forced conversions, wouldn't you think that following in the footsteps of Charlemagne and William the Conqueror, these religious minorities would have been wiped out and forced to become Muslim over time? That never happened.

There are many places where Islam spread simply through trade and not by the sword. Our northern neighbour Indonesia is a perfect example of a nation where Islam reached, not by the sword, but through the good conduct of Arab traders who were trading with the Indonesians. The Indian Subcontinent is a mixed bag; some of the early Islamic conquerors were no more or less brutal than any other militant warriors during the early Middle Ages. For the most part, the Sufis who introduced Islam in areas now spread across Afghanistan, Pakistan and Northern India were peaceful missionaries, not militant conquerors.

Remember that prior to the British Empire's arrival in India, the dominant ruling elite wasn't Hindus, they were the Muslim Mughal Empire. That's whom the Brits took over from. Again, I say, if the Muslim rulers of India were so bent on forced conversions, you would think Hinduism, the world's only major pagan religion left, would have been cast to the archives of history. Just as other pagan religions have disappeared in other parts of the world — just look at what Christianity did to them in Europe.

In short, Islam does not force people to convert. The whole point is to believe after being convinced of the proof of Islam. And if someone considers it, and remains unconvinced, then there is no compulsion on that person. There is a famous verse in Surah Al-Kafiroon in the Quran that says, 'lakum deenukum waliya deen' which means, 'to you be your religion, to me be mine'. That was the essence with which I grew up and that is the essence with which most normal Muslims grow up.

Female Genital Mutilation

The topic of Female Genital Mutilation or FGM has been discussed to death by the critics of Islam. Often the best way to find out whether a given practice is or isn't acceptable to a group of people is to simply ask them.

Ask any Muslim, of any sect, school of thought, denomination, any ethnic background or social status what they think of Female Genital Mutilation. The resounding majority will be completely weirded out at the fact that you're even asking them that question. They will react as if it is a no brainer that FGM cannot possibly be mandated within Islam.

Female Genital Mutilation is a highly backward and problematic cultural practice. It is just that — a cultural practice. It is quite prevalent in tribal East African societies, most notably around the Horn of Africa. In countries like Ethiopia, Djibouti, Eritrea or parts of Egypt, and Somalia, it remains a cultural practice among the less educated people in these countries, irrespective of what religious background they are.[88] Even the Christians of East Africa partake in this practice and plenty of mainstream Muslim jurists and scholars have ruled against the torturous practice. FGM isn't the same as male circumcision, which is in fact mandated by both Judaism and

Islam as a symbolic representation of God's covenant with Abraham. No such thing is required of young Muslim girls.

Plenty of Muslim scholars have ruled or spoken out against this practice. Most notably, in November 2006, Islamic scholars from all over the world convened at the Islamic Al-Azhar University in Cairo to discuss female genital mutilation and unanimously decided to ban the practice.

Professor Ali Goma, the Grand Mufti of Egypt, stated, "The female genital circumcision practiced today harms women psychologically and physically. Therefore, the practice must be stopped in support of one of the highest values of Islam, namely to do no harm to another – in accordance with the commandment of the Prophet Mohammed 'Accept no harm and do no harm to another'. Moreover, this is seen as punishable aggression against humankind".[89]

Likewise, renowned Islamic scholar Yussuf Al-Qaradawi rules that "There is no doubt that the four sources of Islam (Quran, Sunnah, Consensus and Analogy) have no evidence that requires or recommends this practice [...] Therefore, this practice and all allowed acts that bring about damages must be stopped [...] Based on what we said, we consider that circumcision or cutting a part of woman's body without medical care, according to the current way of practice and without justification, is not permitted and is illegal. It enters in the aspect of changing God's creation which is a work of the devil and it is not permitted by God".[90] These opinions of authentic Islamic scholars cannot be ignored. They bear proof that FGM is not a practice endorsed by Islam.

Honour Killings

Before we delve into this topic, let's be clear what we actually mean when we use this term. So, an 'honour killing' is the idea that if a woman from your family (let's say a sister, a wife, a daughter) commits a sexual act which damages the community reputation of the family, that woman has to be put to death. Of course, these practices are backward. Sadly, they do take place, but Islam does not endorse them.

The fact is: no one in Islam can be killed for a crime that cannot be proven in an authentic Sharia Court. And the burden of proof in Islam is the testimony of four adult male witnesses. To put it simply, those who commit honour killings are going against the authentic teachings of Islam. It really is that simple. Remember, that a consistent theme throughout this book is that with legalistic religions such as Judaism and Islam, you cannot simply grab one obscure passage from Holy Scripture and interpret the way you want to.

There are centuries upon centuries worth of scholarly commentaries, and exegeses, produced by experts who devoted their entire lifetimes debating every sentence and verse, working out the most accurate way in which to apply God's law on earth. This scholarly literature, as I have consistently argued, relies upon a system of common consensus. So, these consensus-based verdicts or *fatwahs* cannot be disregarded just like that.

In Islam's case, no mainstream verdict recommends a woman be put to death for bringing dishonour upon the family. University of Sydney cultural expert Professor Sahar Amer has pointed out that Islam has been wrongfully accused of inciting people to engage in honour killings and female genital mutilation. These are not the standard practices in Islam. She goes on to add that, "In the Quran it says very clearly, that if you kill a single human being, it's the same as if you had killed all of humanity".[91]

Likewise, Professor Karl Roberts who specialises in policing and criminal justice at the Western Sydney University points out that assertions about Islam and honour killings are false. He notes that the concept of honour killing, "...seems very much related to cultural belief systems rather than religion" and "There is no part of the Quran that talks about honour as being a fundamental thing".[92]

There have been instances where a husband, father or brother of a woman who was caught having an affair feels she has brought shame and dishonour upon the family, so they end up murdering the person. These cases need to be treated the same way as we would treat any other conventional murder case, without assuming more than we need to.

Remember our discussion from the earlier section about how American society assassinating four *male* Presidents doesn't become automatic proof that American society has a problem with males? It's important we avoid assuming more than we really need to. There have been plenty of cases of jealous husbands and boyfriends murdering their partners in the civilised Western world as well. These murders happen because human beings are flawed. Not because some grand ideology demands them. Islam preaches the opposite.

Taqiyah: Can Muslims lie?

There is a persistent perception among the critics of Islam that Muslims are allowed to lie. This is emphatically untrue. I want to lay this out from the very outset for your peace of mind. My goal in writing this book is to ensure that no part of your curiosity or criticism is left unsatisfied by the time you're done reading it. So, the rest of this section will comprehensively address what *taqiyah* is and isn't, so that you understand how this false perception came about in the first instance. Those who grew up as Jews and Christians may recall, there's the story of Prophet Abraham in the Bible. When Abraham goes to Egypt with his wife Sarah, he knows the Pharaoh had a tradition of killing husbands and sleeping with their wives as captives. So, when asked, whether Sarah was Abraham's wife, he lies and replies she was his sister instead. This saved both his life and her honour. That, right there, is taqiyah.

During the Second World War in Germany, the Nazis often didn't know how to tell apart a Jew from a non-Jew, especially when the Jewish person was secular, and didn't dress like an Orthodox Jew with black Hasidic clothing and the distinctive hat. The Nazis often asked the Jews to identify themselves publicly. If they answered truthfully and confirmed they were Jews, they were taken away to concentration camps, tortured and murdered by the Nazi regime. Some Jews in these circumstances would deny being Jewish in order to save their lives. Were they practising taqiyah? Yes – and good on them for doing so. There is nothing more important than ensuring our own survival as well as that of our families and loved ones.

There is nothing more to the concept of taqiyah than Abraham in Egypt or a Jew in Nazi Germany. The public perception Muslims practice some sort of ritualistic lying is entirely fictional and baseless. It should also be noted that even this level of taqiyah by necessity to save one's life is more common among Shi'ites than it is among Sunnis.

Almost all credible scholars of Islam have ruled against conventional lying for the sake of lying. Unless your life is under a threat, you are not permitted to lie in Islam. This is the opinion of jurists and scholars from all credible schools of thought within Islam. Even the Quran strictly warns against bearing a false witnesses, or lying by stressing, "...And do not mix the truth with falsehood or conceal the truth while you know it."[93]

Professor Shakira Hussein cites the Oxford dictionary definition of taqiyyah as, "precautionary denial of religious belief in the face of potential persecution". In her ABC article titled, *'The Myth of the Lying Muslim: Taqiyya and the Racialisation of Muslim Identity'* Professor Hussein argues that in the world since September 11, the tendency to assume Muslims practice ritualistic lying has become a growing trend. She points out there is no basis to this.[94]

The point we have to bear in mind is that anyone, regardless of which religion or culture one follows, would be prepared to lie if their lives were in danger and the only thing that could save you was a lie. Islam being a realistic religion has made sure people who are put through this kind of a situation are not punished for their lifesaving lies. There is nothing more to it than that.

Does Islam condone slavery?

The idea that Islam condones slavery is not as widespread among the critics of Islam as some of the other issues I have tried to address in these myth busting sections. But I have seen plenty of people in online comments making this allegation. As with every other issue, I believe this too needs to be addressed.

We often forget that for most of human history, slavery was a universal norm; quite literally every culture in the world practiced it. Most of the founding fathers of the United States of America were slave owners. This is somewhat ironic considering that the words of the US declaration of independence states, "We hold these truths to be self-evident that all men are created equal".[95] Clearly, they did not think black Africans were equal to them at the time.

Africa was and, in some ways, remains a deeply divided continent. It is full of many different ethnic groups and religious communities that often have very complex relationships with each other. During the heyday of the Atlantic slave trade during the 1700s, African tribal warlords often captured men and women from rival tribes and sold them off to any buyers who wanted them.

In a pre-industrial age where machines hadn't yet been invented and agriculture formed the economic backbone of world societies, the value of manual labour could not be underestimated. Africans were perceived as tall, muscular and in high endurance. Others from imperialistic nations that were busy setting up colonies around the world found African slaves to be very useful, especially for work on cotton and sugar plantations.

The slave owners weren't always Europeans. Often, they were Arabs, who happened to be Muslim. Slavery is as ancient as humanity itself. Going even further back, the Romans enslaved Africans and used them as gladiators in Roman amphitheatres and colosseums for the entertainment of the crowds.

To put it simply, slavery is a scourge and an immoral practice. There is no doubt about that. None of us would ever appreciate being kidnapped against our will, sold to some buyer and be forced to serve them. Yet it has taken humans thousands of years to realise this. The good news is we humans are an ever-evolving species.

But for thousands of years, humans across all major cultures practiced slavery in some shape or form. As a product of the 7th century, Islam was no different. Islam encouraged slave owners to treat their slaves with dignity and respect. Prophet Muhammad himself urged the early Muslims to treat their slaves with justice. When Prophet Muhammad saw that Bilal, an Abyssinian slave, was being treated harshly by his master at the time, he bought Bilal and treated him as an equal. Bilal went on to becoming one of Muhammad's great companions and the first ever person to recite the Islamic call to prayer the *Adhan* at the Holy Kaaba in Islam's history.

Just as the West had its champions of the abolition movement in William Wilberforce, in Britain and Abraham Lincoln in the United States, Islam too has built consensus over time that slavery has no place today. Of the 57 Muslim majority nations, not one participates in slave trade practices and no Muslim community living in the West practices nor endorses slavery.

Islam's historical attitude towards the practice should be understood considering the norms of the past, the same way that we would understand Western attitudes towards it. Anyone, anywhere in the world who still practices slavery is going against Islam and the civilised norms of today's world. Every credible Islamic scholar would confirm as much.

Does Islam tolerate gays and lesbians?

Western society has come a long way in how it treats same sex relationships. The fact that less than two years ago, same sex marriages were still outlawed in Australia is a difficult thing for many to come to terms with. It's even more difficult to realise that only thirty years ago, homosexuality itself was considered a crime. Islam prescribes no penalty or punishment for gays or lesbians who do not publicly display homosexual behaviour. As is the case with fornication and adultery, Sharia Law only prescribes punishment for those caught in the act publicly by at least four adult male witnesses. In a nutshell, Islam's problem is not with homosexuality per se, it is with its ability to encourage and normalise homosexual behaviour in the eyes of others in the wider society. Islam has no issue whatsoever with the gays and lesbians who keep their homosexual activities private.

Note that Islamic history has traditionally not been dismissive of homosexuals. Prophet Muhammad's wife Umm Salama, for instance, had a gay male servant in their home.[96] During the Islamic Golden Age, homosexuality was openly spoken and written about. Great Arab poet Abu Nuwas openly talked about homoerotic fantasies.[97] American historian George Haggerty notes that Abu Nuwas was openly gay and his poems full of homoerotic fantasies about his male lovers. He outlived most of his critics and managed to go down in Islamic history as one of the great entertainers of the Golden Age.[98] Another gay Muslim was a contemporary of Abu Nuwas. Caliph Al-Amin was the openly gay son of Caliph Harun Al-Rashid. Muslim historian At-Tabari notes that the gay caliph fell in love with one of his male servants Kauthar. The Caliph's mother often attempted to lure her gay son by fashioning young women, but the Caliph Al-Amin remained proudly gay his whole life.[99] Likewise, Afghan Muslim conqueror Mahmud Ghaznavi was known for his love of another male, Malik Ayaz.[100]

In one of the most celebrated Muslim autobiographies of all time, Mughal Emperor Babur speaks of his own attraction to a male he saw at a bazaar during the 1500s. During the 1700s a writer by the name of Dargah Quli Khan travelling through the Muslim parts of the Indian Subcontinent described how prevalent homosexuality was in those days. He describes that male prostitutes openly sought clients in public places.[101] This is not the image most Westerners would have of the Islamic world when contemplating it today.

Ironically, the Ottomans decriminalised homosexuality in 1858. By contrast the British Empire two years later created the Indian Penal Code 377, which proceeded to outlaw homosexuality in British India, which includes the territories of today's Pakistan, India and Bangladesh.[102] The Ottoman reforms towards homosexuality were led by Grand Vizier Mustafa Resid Pasha who was himself gay, although he was twice married to women and had five children.

Caliph Al-Hakam II Al-Mustansir, who was known for keeping a male harem[103] guided Islamic Spain known as *Al-Andalus* to the peak of its glory just before the turn of the first millennium. He was apparently more attracted to men than women during his youth. Despite having a vast harem of blonde concubines (the Umayyad caliphs of Spain were fond of the Basque people), he failed to get any of them pregnant. This of course was problematic from a dynastic perspective. In the end, the story goes, they dressed a Basque concubine up as a boy and named him Ja'far (her original name was Subh). She succeeded in giving Al-Hakam a son, the future caliph Hisham II. After Al-Hakam died this son proved to be grossly incompetent, and Subh proved to be a rather imperious Queen Mother.[104]

In more recent times, Pakistan, which is seen as a socially conservative Islamic nation, has a large transgender population. The Pakistani government has passed a law guaranteeing basic rights for transgender citizens. Discrimination by employers and private business owners is outlawed. Pakistani government documents such as National Identification Cards, passports and driver's licenses allow for transgender people not to identify as either male or female, but as a blend of both genders.[105] Contrast this with some of the rhetoric we hear in Australia from our own conservative politicians especially with respect to the whole debate around 'Safe Schools'.[106] It makes Pakistan seem like a tolerant country.

It should be clear enough by this stage that Islamic history is not intrinsically homophobic. If anything, it has been quite accepting of homosexual conduct so long as the conduct wasn't evangelical in its outlook or looking to promote homosexuality as some sort of a social norm. It is fair to assume that Islam operated on a 'what happens in private, stays in private' principle.

There are, of course, individuals who find homosexuality uncomfortable. Those individuals exist in all human societies, not just in Muslim communities. But we shouldn't let their existence deter us from appreciating Islam's rich and generally tolerant history towards gays and lesbians. Of course, no culture is perfect, and I said at the start, even we in the West until recently had criminalised homosexuality. Islamic civilisation is also not perfect, but when we look at examples of gay caliphs, the Pakistani government's acceptance of a third gender category, and the Prophet Muhammad's own household having a gay servant, it forces us to realise that Islamic history hasn't been altogether as homophobic as some critics of Islam might like us to believe.

Does Islam promote polygamy?

Polygamy is the term used to refer to a man marrying more than one wife. It obviously sounds odd to our modern ears, but polygamy has been, at some point, the standard practice for most of human history across almost all cultures of the world. The Biblical prophet Abraham had multiple wives, Sarah, the mother of the Jewish people through son Isaac and Hagar, the mother of the Arab people through son Ishmael. Likewise, the most central lawgiving figure of Judaism, the prophet Moses himself had two wives Zipporah and Tharbis.

The Bible notes that the Jewish King Solomon, also known for building the first Jewish Temple in Jerusalem was known for having 700 wives and 300 concubines. Mentioning these examples is important. Abraham, Moses and Solomon are not fictional characters from some novel set in the distant past, these are believed to be actual prophets appointed by God himself to lead the Jewish people. Jews, Christians and Muslims all believe in their existence. Their names are often cited today to prove Jewish historical connection to the land of Israel.

As an ancient cultural practice that was once the norm in the ancient Middle East, polygamy was inherited by Islam at the time of its advent in the 7th century. The pagan Arabs before Islam were an indulgent and socially degenerate people, their polygamous practices knew no bounds. A man often took on dozens of wives as a display of power, as if to suggest the greater the number of wives and concubines, the more of a man he was. After Islam took over much of Arabia, it limited this practice and put a maximum cap of four wives only. This was a relatively later development in the Prophet's 23-year long career from the ages of 40 until his death at 63.

A key factor for still allowing polygamy rather than altogether banning it was the surplus of women compared to men in the Arabian population. There were more women than men in those days. If each man in Arabia during the 7th century were to take on a single wife, there would still be a massive surplus of women left without a husband.

The fact that this male to female ratio was disproportionate at the time can also be gauged from another crucial point mentioned in a different section of this book. The Arabs were burying their first-born daughters alive until they had a son. This again was a measure to reduce the number of women through a morally repugnant practice.

This helps us understand that Islam allowing polygamy had both cultural and sociological reasons behind it. The cultural reasons came from the polygamous context of the Jewish Old Testament upon which Islam was based. And the sociological reasons came from the gender imbalance between too few males and too many women in Arabia at the time.

Over the centuries, Islamic rulers often did take on multiple wives because they were wealthy enough to afford the same. Islam highly encourages that if a man takes on multiple wives, he must make sure he is able to do justice between them. The traditional view among scholars has been that since most people are incapable of doing justice to multiple wives, they should stick to only one. That has, in fact, been the norm for Muslim societies.

The total incidence of polygamous marriages is extremely low in Muslim populations worldwide and even lower in Muslim communities living in the West. It is not a practice that is on the rise; rather it is a practice that is decreasing. Most Muslim women these days would not allow for their husbands to be shared by a third person. This is a universal attitude among women of all cultures.

Now remains the question of why women can't have multiple husbands? Answering this question isn't as difficult as some might think. Traditional societies have always drawn a distinction between the roles of women and men. Islamic society isn't unique in this. In the hunter-gatherer period of history, men would go out, hunt an animal, skin it, roast it on fire, prepare the meal for the family and women would raise children.

This was the natural order of history across all types of humans everywhere in the world. It is because women were the ones who bore pregnancy and childbirth, as opposed to men, traditional societies came to conclude that a woman taking on multiple husbands would make it impossible to differentiate who the father of the child was. Either way, polygamy is not a common practice among most Muslims worldwide as things stand today.

Still, as far as the Muslim community in Australia is concerned, sadly polygamy does still occur from time to time. There have been several cases of it. People have reportedly taken on multiple spouses and even end up claiming additional welfare for it.

While our legal system is based on bigamy, meaning a man and a woman can only take one spouse at a time, many people find loopholes in the system to declare multiple partners in *de facto* relationships. This shouldn't be happening. It is illegal. It is immoral and it is un-Australian.

Hijab, Niqab and Burqa: What's Islamic and what isn't?

We must begin by clarifying what's what. Hijab is the head covering comparable to what Catholic Nuns have on their heads where no part of their hair is showing. Niqab is a face veil. A Burqa is the complete head-to-toe garment. To cut to the chase on this topic, Islam absolutely does not require a full head-to-toe Burqa. It is only advocated by a minority of Muslims and has become more of a cultural practice than a religiously sanctioned one.

Scholars from credible schools of thought generally agree that the

Hijab is obligatory. But it must be noted that Muslim women are free to choose whether they wish to wear it. The idea they are forced to wear the Hijab by their husbands is far from reality. This only happens in the vast minority of cases.

The proof of this can be seen by looking around the Islamic world at some of those famous Muslim leaders whom we mentioned in the section that concerns the status of women in Islam. Turkish Prime Minister Tansu Ciller did not wear a Hijab, nor did Megawati Sukarnoputri the President of Indonesia, nor does Queen Rania of Jordan. Benazir Bhutto of Pakistan used to don a cloth called 'dupatta' in the Subcontinent, which isn't exactly a Hijab as it still shows the front fringes of the woman's hair. Bangladeshi Prime Ministers Khaleda Zia and Sheikh Hasina both also wore a dupatta, not a Hijab.

It is entirely up to the woman. I have never worn the Hijab myself. I've never felt that I was any less of a Muslim. But, I wouldn't rule out starting to wear it as I get older. Time will tell. It's nobody's business to care, just as we do not care about Orthodox Jewish women and Catholic Nuns who also choose to cover their hair as long as the face is shown because the face is the marker of our identity.

Muslim women are free to choose how they decide to fashion their head coverings. In this section, I have cited examples of countless prominent Muslim women around the world to make that point clear.

Can Muslim women initiate a divorce?

The answer is yes. We discussed in the status of women section earlier that Prophet Muhammad uplifted the status of Muslim women, relative to the norms of the 7th century, and one of the big reforms he underwent was to allow women to be able to initiate a divorce. That was previously not the case in pre-Islamic Arabia.

As a result of this reform, Muslim women can go to the *Qadi* or *Hakim* (Islamic terms for marriage celebrants) and file for a divorce if her husband is not fulfilling his obligations, or not providing for her and the family, not offering enough protection, or not able to give sexual gratification. A woman can also file for divorce if her husband abuses her.

Is Apostasy Punishable by Death?

Among the most common criticisms Islam attracts is that it kills ex-Muslims for leaving Islam. As I have argued throughout this book, there is often a disconnect between Islam as interpreted and prescribed by Muslim scholars and Islam as often practiced by misguided Muslims. The minute we understand this divide, we start to understand a large part of the point behind the 'myths and facts' sections of this book. It is true that often, Muslim regimes and communities around the world end up acting more hardcore than what Islam actually requires of them.

The issue of apostasy is really no different. The general perception among critics is that Islam necessarily prescribes the death penalty for anyone who leaves it. In actual fact, there is a difference of opinion among scholars on this subject. When I was growing up, I recall mum teaching us the famous hadith as a kid when someone was forgiven for leaving Islam. According to this famous hadith, a Bedouin Arab converts to Islam, then gets sick and comes to the Prophet Muhammad and announces he no longer wishes to go ahead with his conversion. The Prophet refused to accept the cancellation of his original pledge to Islam three times in a row. The Bedouin then goes away and that's the end of the story. Nobody was hurt or punished.[107]

In other words, there was no action taken against the guy for leaving Islam. Islamic jurisprudence is based on precedents. The overwhelming majority of Muslim scholars today do not in fact prescribe capital punishment to those who leave Islam. Famous Islamic jurist Ibn Taymiyyah held that apostasy was not an extreme crime and did not prescribe the death penalty. And for the record, he was supposed to be one of the hardliners of his day.

To see proof of this, visit any Sharia court in Jordan or Pakistan and you will see it with your own eyes. It must be remembered that the traditional death penalty for apostasy can only be carried out by an official Caliph or the Imam of an official Islamic state, and it is related to treason or sedition against the state. So in other words, if there is a caliphate in the Islamic world and a person renounces their faith, nothing happens. If the person acts in sedition against the interests of the state, then after formal trial and failure to repent, capital punishment may apply. This is the same as in the United States where sedition by a military official that compromises the security and interests of the United States or its citizens is punishable by death.

The idea is to protect the integrity of the wider community. Every great regime and empire of the past had some form of a capital punishment for its major dissidents and traitors. What we would call sedition is literally the equivalent of apostasy from a religion. So while mainstream authentic Islam does not necessarily enforce capital punishment to all and every case of somebody exiting the faith, there certainly have been select regimes in the past who, much like any Western military that pronounces capital punishment for sedition, has chosen to do the same.

Some Muslim regimes continue to do so today. This does not mean that those practices are necessarily encouraged by authentic Islamic scripture or jurisprudence. The issue is far more complex than that. Scholarly opinions are far more divided than that. And consensus today is that the practice is not Islamic.

4

Guidance for Muslims in the West

I am well aware that I don't have all the answers to all of the problems on this complex issue. That said, if we are ever to see steps towards progress, we must first establish enough harmony between Muslims and non-Muslims to have calm, rational discussions. If we are committed to creating a world of peaceful co-existence, we need to try to understand each other's perspectives. I want to conclude my book by pulling together the problem, which faces us — with some detailed insights into how we may be able to make change.

Australia, We Have a Problem

We began this book by establishing that not all Muslims are terrorists, but the vast majority of present-day terrorists are Muslims. There are, of course, exceptions to this. Recently, we've also seen a rise in white nationalists terrorism. The Christchurch massacre that left 50 innocent people murdered in cold blood in 2019 is a horrific example of this.

Without a doubt, acts of terrorism are inexcusable, no matter who commits them. The fact that so many Muslims have chosen to go down this path is troubling. It's not surprising that so many of us struggle to come to terms with this inconvenient reality.

Westerners are frightened, for obvious reasons.

As far as Westerners are concerned, their societies have opened their arms wide open, let so many Muslim migrants into Western countries and granted them the same democratic rights as ordinary Westerners. For a small minority within that minority of Muslims to commit acts of terror against civilians in the host country is despicable. The Westerner's view of terrorism is completely understandable.

On the other side, Muslims are equally frightened because every time acts of terrorism occur, they fear there will be a backlash against their community. These anxieties are not unfounded either. There have been many such instances where Muslim women wearing a headscarf have been shouted at publicly with insulting slogans and mosques have been vandalised.

While I'm not of the view that this kind of a backlash is based on some irrational phobia of Islam, we do have to acknowledge it is a rational fear, it still exists and continues to irritate the Muslims who do not support terrorism in the slightest.

Though mainstream Westerners and moderate Muslims both have a shared concern over terrorism, especially Islamist terrorism, sometimes it's difficult to see the commonality of the concerns. This is because Westerners and Muslims often hold clashing political outlooks on world events. The response ends up reflecting that difference.

Far too much of the public discussion on terrorism in the West revolves around journalists asking Islamic community leaders to repeatedly condemn terrorism. The leader either refuses to do so or does it while concurrently claiming that terrorism is only a reaction to Western military intervention in Muslim lands.

Perhaps the best-known example of this is the 2014 encounter between Hizb ut-Tahrir representative Wassim Doureihi and ABC's Lateline host Emma Alberici.[108] She began the interview by asking him whether him or his organisation supported the actions of ISIS. Doureihi simply refused to give a straight yes or no response to that question. It must be noted that while the ABC has the reputation of being quite left of centre; many of its most senior journalists are often sympathetic to ethnic and religious minorities, including the Islamic community.

All that Doureihi had to do was reciprocate and give a simple yes or no response to Alberici's question. Chances are, then, she would have gladly provided him the opportunity to discuss what he wanted to with regard to US military intervention in the Middle East. As a matter of fact, she even says so herself about halfway through that interview.

Alberici points out to Doureihi that the point he is trying to make has in fact been made by many experts around the world. All she wanted him to do was to give a clear-cut response whether his organisation, Hizb ut-Tahrir Australia, supports or condemns the violent tactics of ISIS. He simply failed to do that. By the time he reluctantly pointed out his organisation does in fact condemn those acts as per many press releases on their website, the interview had soured, and the remainder was never going to be harmonious or productive.

This was a missed opportunity as far as Doureihi was concerned. What's disappointing is, he's not the only one to miss such an opportunity. Wherever in the West there are Muslim community leaders and curious journalists looking to provide coverage to the topic of Islam and terrorism, these questions will continue to be asked. I acknowledged right at the beginning of this book that Westerners cannot simply be blamed for the fear and suspicion, which they often hold for Muslims. In a post-September 11 world, these anxieties are quite understandable.

Dealing with the public's concerns about Islam is nobody else's responsibility but that of prominent Muslim leaders. If large numbers of Westerners continue to think negatively about Islam, this isn't so much a case of them being "racist" or "islamophobic", it has more to do with the fact that those Muslim leaders must be doing their job wrong. This antagonistic approach is something Muslim community leaders must change.

Thankfully, not every single leader in the Islamic community is like Wassim Doureihi. There are some good leaders who do go out of their way to unequivocally condemn terrorism. I worry that their voices aren't heard loud enough.

At this point, it is important to remember that Islam does not have a central authority; there is no Vatican City or a papacy in Islam. This is truer of Sunni Islam than Shi'ite Islam, which does have a central authority vested in the word of the Grand Ayatollah. But Shi'ite Islam only happens to be the dominant stream of Islam practiced in a single nation state, and that is Iran. For the rest of the Sunni world, Islamic rulings operate on a consensus basis as explained in the middle parts of the book.

There isn't one single authority figure in Sunni Islam, equivalent to the Pope in Catholicism, who could come out and issue some sort of a binding official condemnation of Islamist terrorism. No single person has the authority to speak on another's behalf in Islamic thought.

That said, there are many individual scholars within Sunni Islam around the world, who all form part of a wider Islamic jurisprudential community. They operate a little like the academic community. They do in fact condemn terrorism in their private capacities and do so in the strongest possible terms.

In 2014, when ISIS established its caliphate, 100 senior Islamic clerics from around the world issued a joint fatwah against them and condemned their violent methods for bringing about a caliphate. It must be noted that a caliphate itself is something that is part of mainstream Islamic thinking as discussed in the middle section of this book. But that's not to say that every Muslim scholar thinks a caliphate can only be brought about through an armed struggle. Muslim scholarly opinions are split on this matter.

Most scholars do not believe the use of any violent extremist tactics are the correct way to bring about a caliphate.

These 100 senior Islamic clerics addressed their fatwah to ISIS' self-appointed leader, or caliph, Abu Bakr Al-Baghdadi. The text of the fatwah included many explicit statements which most Westerners would sadly never even get to hear about, coming from mainstream Muslim circles.

If Emma Alberici had anyone of these 100 Imams from around the world on her show, she would have had a cooperative and robust discussion on this crucial subject of Islamist terrorism. Unlike Wassim Doureihi who blew the opportunity to do so. This famous fatwah says the following lines that are crucial for our interests to note:[109]

> "It is forbidden in Islam to kill the innocent."
> "It is forbidden in Islam to kill emissaries, ambassadors, and diplomats; hence it is forbidden to kill journalists and aid workers. Jihad in Islam is defensive war."
> "It is forbidden in Islam to harm or mistreat—in any way—Christians or any 'People of the Scripture.'"
> "The re-introduction of slavery is forbidden in Islam. It was abolished by universal consensus"
> "It is forbidden in Islam to force people to convert"
> "It is forbidden in Islam to deny women their rights"
> "It is forbidden in Islam to torture people"
> "It is forbidden in Islam to declare a caliphate without consensus from all Muslims"

The Muslim scholars who signed this fatwah were from more nation-states than can be listed in a single paragraph, but I'll try: Argentina, Egypt, Chad, Nigeria, Jordan, Turkey, Yemen, Palestine, United States, Malaysia, Portugal, United Arab Emirates, Indonesia, Morocco, Tunisia, Saudi Arabia, Italy, Bulgaria, Sweden, United Kingdom, Germany, Bosnia, Netherlands, Iraq, North Sudan, France, Pakistan, Canada, Kurdistan, Kosovo, Syria and Uzbekistan.

For a religion that does not have a papacy or a pope, moderate Islam does a good job of coming out to condemn terrorism.

These condemnations are not a one-off; they are actually rather frequent. Every so often, as Islamist terrorist incidents happen to peak around the world, various groups of prominent Islamic community leaders do tend to come out and issue similar condemnations time and time again.

Another classic example of this happening was in early 2018 when 70 of the most eminent Islamic clerics around the world did exactly the same.[110] Likewise, American sociologist and professor of Middle Eastern and Islamic studies at the University of North Carolina, Dr Charles Kurzman, has conducted an extensively study into the staggering numbers of fatwas condemning Islamic terrorism.

Kurzman's research is widely available on the Internet and lists the names of every single credible Imam and literally dozens of Islamic organisations within the United States and elsewhere, which have partaken in these condemnations.[111] Similarly, the website 'Global Condemnations of ISIS/ISIL' lists hundreds of fatwas from mainstream Islamic scholars and organisations condemning terrorism.[112]

It's clear that the problem isn't that there isn't enough condemnation of Islamic terrorism from within Islamic communities. The issue is that there seems to be a group of theologically motivated Islamic scholars who already are issuing condemnation upon condemnation, one fatwah after another, to do exactly that, yet at the same time, there are the self-appointed community leaders, who may not necessarily be scholars, who tend to refuse to issue those condemnations in plain terms.

This confuses the public. The trouble with the non-scholarly leaders of the Islamic community is they tend to not want the entire discussion on Islamist terrorism to be exclusively stalled by demands for repeated condemnations, and nothing else of substance. As we saw the trend from the Doureihi encounter with Alberici, he was only interested in, rightly or wrongly, externalising the blame for the failures of the Islamic world on the West.

There is a reason why this tends to happen. Remember that many Muslims obviously do have their own political outlook, which often does overlap with what Islamist terrorists are supposed to be fighting for.

This is the major reason why prominent Muslim figures like Doureihi get so worked up if they are asked to repeatedly condemn Islamist terrorism. You would notice the condemnation part takes up around 10 to 20% of their airtime, while the remaining 80 to 90% of the airtime is consumed debating US foreign policy, Zionism or the State of Israel and the occupation of the Palestinians.

This is why I said earlier that while mainstream Westerners and Muslims both share the same concerns about the rise of terrorism, they still have clashing political priorities. Since the average Westerner is generally fairly indifferent to things like European colonialism, US foreign policy, the Palestinian issue, or the Iraq War, it's easier for them to simply issue a condemnation and leave it at that.

For leaders of Muslim communities, especially the not-so scholarly ones living in the West, the issue clearly isn't as easy as that. After all, they too want to see the Palestinian issue resolved. They too want to see the Americans taking greater precaution before invading another Muslim country.

After all, no weapons of mass destruction were found in Iraq last time we went in, and thousands of civilian casualties resulted from that war. This doesn't mean that Muslim community leaders necessarily support terrorism. Rather, it means they and the Islamists have some common motives. So, while you have hundreds of Muslim scholars issuing fatwas against suicide bombings, stabbings and the mowing down of pedestrians, there are no fatwas against the underlying motives of the terrorists.

It follows, then, that when Muslims are asked to condemn terrorism, of course they pay lip service to such expectations, but deep down many of them do feel that they're the ones being treated unfairly. This mindset must change. In turn, Westerners don't intend to corner Muslims into such discussions, nor do most Muslims necessarily want to be rationalising acts of terrorism. Each party has such opposite worldviews that such awkward clashes, like those between Doureihi and Alberici, just end up emerging naturally.

Counterterrorism experts in the West have long argued that normal people do not turn towards terrorism. If we look closely at some of the profiles and biographical details of the culprits that carry out such attacks, those details would stand to challenge such a proposition. Many of these people are about as normal as anyone can be. Sure it is true that some terrorists probably do suffer from a mental illness of some sort, but there is no way on earth anyone can argue that most terrorists are mentally ill.

Surely not, most of them know exactly what they're doing. They have their fixed political worldviews, and they know exactly how to make a loud noise in front of the international community to get to where they want to be. Of course, and perhaps we should say fortunately, it is a good thing that terrorist regimes like the Taliban, Al-Qaeda and ISIS have failed in recent times.

But given that the anti-American, anti-Israel sentiments that are widely exploited by these terrorist organisations in order to attract more recruits remain highly prevalent among mainstream Muslims, the best advice I could offer Muslims is to think more critically about the role of America in the modern world.

Unless the Muslim mindset is cleansed of these deeply entrenched conspiracy theories and one-sided interpretations of past and present events around the globe, I highly doubt that we as a society will be able to permanently put an end to Islamist terrorism.

It must be noted, while I was lucky that my own family never really held anti-America anti-Israel views, I must admit I have come across many Muslim families that did. What I have found throughout my life is that the Muslim contempt towards the West and its allies isn't always grounded in religious theology.

This helps us understand why so many of the more learned scholars have no trouble issuing all those fatwas condemning terrorism. If anything, it happens to be the non-scholarly leaders of the Islamic community that seem to have all the problems with the West and its allies.

It is true that it's a common error on the part of Westerners to presume that the most radical of Muslims are generally more devout. This isn't usually true. I would argue, the ones who end up getting radicalised are usually the least religious ones. We should note though that those who run these terrorist organisations from the top, such as the leaders of Al-Qaeda or ISIS, are most definitely devoutly religious, but the average foot soldier that allows himself to get radicalised usually does so for political reasons.

This distinction between the theological and political aspects is crucial. The person who ends up being radicalised is essentially only a handful of notches up from the rest of mainstream Muslims. The best advice I can give to Muslims who find themselves tempted to go down that path is this: Remember, nobody has put a gun to your head and forced you to come live in the West. You made that choice voluntarily.

It's fair to assume that if any Muslim chooses to leave his or her home behind to resettle in Australia, he or she does so because there are certain freedoms and options available here that aren't otherwise available back home. This is an absolutely non-negotiable self-evident fact. If anyone says Australia is worse than or, at the most, equal to their country of origin, that would defy all logic. It would beg the question, if Australia isn't in fact much better than your home country then why did you come here in the first place? It makes no sense to migrate from one average country to another.

Surely this happens because there is that underlying belief, whether consciously realised or not, that these Western countries offer a better life. It is too often forgotten that these Western countries and their allies which remain migrant hotspots for Muslims are all part of the same US-led world order that Muslims generally hold responsible for invading their countries.

This again begs the question, if the West is so complicit in the suffering of Muslims, why do so many Muslims migrate to the West? Why not move to China, India, Japan, the oil-rich Gulf States, or Sub-Saharan Africa? You would think the options were limitless. This is where we need to call out the hypocrisy of too many Islamic community leaders. These people are responsible for the occasional friction that we see between so many well-intentioned Westerners and equally well-intentioned Muslims.

Then there is the argument about assimilation. It is too often assumed that terrorism happens because recruited terrorists have failed to assimilate into Australian society. The problem here isn't simply a lack of assimilation. The issue here goes way deeper than that. No one has yet been able to properly explain it. This again is another reason why this book was necessary.

So, whether we are talking about Muhammad Elomar who became infamous for having his young child hold up the severed head of a slain human in Syria, or Dr Tareq Kamleh who gave up his medical career in Adelaide to go join ISIS, the overwhelming majority of those who fled the country to fight with the ISIS death cult were actually Australian-born Australian-educated fully Westernised youngsters who spoke flawless English without a foreign accent. They grew up with plenty of white Australian friends and often went out partying hard.

Does that sound to you like lack of assimilation was the problem? Surely not. These people were as Aussie as anyone and yet still made the life choices that they did. This compels us to realise that the real reasons for radicalisation is more complex than what we currently understand.

Not to mention, there have been many cases of born and bred white Australians who also allowed themselves to be radicalised. The case of Melbourne teenager Jake Bilardi is one such example.[113] Was lack of assimilation the problem for him? Surely not. We need to understand that some people just choose to go down this destructive path when they feel whoever they identify to be their people are under attack.

The assumption that people are being radicalised because they are failing to integrate or assimilate in our society is way too oversimplified. Too often when people talk about integration or assimilation, the truth is that they have no idea what those words even mean. This issue is dealt with in more detail in the next section.

The fact is that you can assimilate a person into any culture, but that doesn't guarantee you'll switch his or her loyalties. Nor does it mean you will redefine their radius of extended sympathies. What this is referring to is who they consider to be 'their people' and whom they're essentially prepared to express their compassion for.

When natural disasters strike our nation, like the floods in Queensland or the bushfires in Victoria as has often been the case, ordinary Australian hearts go out to the families of the victims, to the point that we, as Australians, often feel obliged to raise funds, donate generously and welcome those affected into our own homes.

To put it simply, this is because they're our people, we feel for our fellow Australians. We feel a sense of responsibility towards the wider community. Indeed, doing all that is what makes us, a nation. But what we have to remember is that not everybody shares the same radius of extended sympathy and compassion. Many different minority communities continue to feel a sense of responsibility towards others who share their identities around the world.

Jewish Australians obviously care for what goes on in Israel regardless of whether they have Israeli citizenship or not. This is completely natural and understandable. It must be duly noted that Jewish Australians are the best example of how your radius of sympathy and compassion can include multiple groups of people without there being any contradiction.

The same goes for Jewish Americans, or Jews living anywhere else in the world. They feel for America, or Britain, or wherever it is that they're living as well as for Israel at the same time without this resulting in any cognitive dissonance whatsoever. If only Muslims could achieve a balanced synthesis between their multiple sympathies, that would be most ideal.

While some migrants put their ethnicity above their religion, others put their religion above their ethnicity. Particularly when Muslims migrate to Western countries, their religious identity goes on to supersede other levels of their identity. So for instance an Australian citizen of Lebanese ancestry may identify as a 'Muslim Australian' instead of 'Lebanese Australian', which then means that they start to feel connected with another Muslim of any ethnic background as part of 'their people'.

Too many Muslims struggle to juggle their loyalties and sympathies between the Australian communities here at home and the community of Muslims abroad, that is, the 'ummah'. They often feel they have to choose one over the other. Whether that's conscious or not, they end up developing a preference for their religious identity over their current Australian nationality.

This point must be clarified. In saying they trade in their national identity with a religious one does not imply that those who make this trade-off are necessarily devout Muslims in the strict religious sense. What it means is that they see their religion as their cultural identity and wear it as a badge of honour irrespective of how ever bad Muslims they may be in practice.

Just as many Christians neither read the Bible nor attend Church on Sundays, the same is true of many Muslims who neither read the Quran nor attend the mosque on Fridays. However, what they do feel is a sense of connection with their broader Islamic civilisational identity.

Instead of living in Australia as simply 'Australians' and showing the same concern for the same things that concern the rest of ordinary Australians, once Muslim Australians define themselves in those terms as 'Muslim Australians' naturally both their loyalty and their radius of extended sympathy gets redrawn in the community's collective mind.

Instead of showing any real concern for those Australians affected by the Queensland floods of 2010/2011[114] or the Victorian bush fires of 2009[115], their concerns and sympathies are instead redirected towards a whole bunch of foreign causes such as the plight of the Palestinians in Gaza[116] or the suffering of the Rohingyas in the Rakhine State in Burma.[117]

To feel this way, you don't necessarily need to be a foreign sounding or a foreign acting citizen of Australia. You could be culturally very well assimilated and still feel greater sympathies for Palestinians and Rohingyas than for Queenslanders and Victorians. You could be like that and still laugh at Australian jokes, enjoy Australian TV shows, attend Australian schools, colleges and universities, or the local country fair, enjoy footy or cricket.

Often the most 'assimilated' highly Westernised Australian Muslims are the ones who go out of their ways to distance themselves from any aspect of Australian nationalism. Even the least patriotic and completely indifferent Australians can usually connect with things like Anzac Day on 25th April or Australia Day on 26th January every year. But the case with those who choose to identify as 'Muslim Australians' is often peculiar and different.

It is one thing to be simply indifferent to Australian nationalism and quite another to actively oppose it. It is fascinating how Australian society welcomes Muslims to become Australians on equal terms, yet so many choose to relegate themselves to a minority status by redrawing the boundaries of their identity and redirecting their national pride elsewhere — often to geographical locations they have never stepped foot on and often end up considering as part of 'their people' those with whom they do not share a language or nationality.

Too often, we tend to assume that when Muslim Australians get radicalised, they are waking up in the morning and reading some obscure violent passage out of the Quran that supposedly mandates violence and then going off and blowing things up. This sort of a view is an oversimplification of the root causes of radicalisation.

Too often, academics have also tried to suggest that radicalisation happens as the result of failure to be properly educated, or due to unemployment or some other form of social inequality and marginalisation.[118] These suggestions may be well-intentioned but they don't suffice to explain why able-bodied, educated and well-integrated men like Dr Tareq Kamleh chose to give up the good life he had to go join the fight.[119]

As we discussed in earlier chapters, creating a theocratic state is not peripheral to Islam, it is, in fact, Islam. There is no doubt many who understand Islam in detail do wish to create a jurisdiction where Islam gets to be the legal system. Throughout history, there were different caliphates in different eras.

The last globally recognised caliphate to exist in the world was the Ottoman Empire that ran its course from 1299 during the Middle Ages until the end of World War I in 1917.[120] Since then, there hasn't been another global Sunni Islamic caliphate on earth. But there have been several attempts to create one — and most of these attempts have tended to be extreme in nature.

The Taliban in Afghanistan attempted to create a caliphate in 1996 from the fallout of the Soviet-Afghan wars and their effort was, at first, tolerated by the United States and later retaliated to, following the events of September 11, 2001. President George W. Bush's 'War on Terror' toppled the Taliban due to their refusal to turn over prime suspect Osama bin Laden.[121]

The second attempt to establish a caliphate through violence was ISIS or 'Daesh' the so-called Islamic State in Syria and Iraq in 2014 from the fallout of the Iraq war on the one hand, and the Arab Spring gone bad in Syria on the other.[122] Insurgent groups operating within Iraq teamed up with the Free Syrian Army across the border to form this quasi-state that was ISIS, which as things currently stand, has largely been degraded and destroyed.[123]

The sort of Westernised Muslims we are talking about are often more likely to succumb to terrorist propaganda magazines than unassimilated ones. These magazines paint a more grisly picture of the political realities within the Islamic world than what is actually the case.

Osama bin Laden's terrorist organisation Al-Qaeda used to run a propaganda publication called The Inspire Magazine. ISIS ran a propaganda publication called the Dabiq magazine.

The purpose of both these publications was to call on Muslims worldwide to do God's will and to help create a Sunni Islamic caliphate. They would often pry on the political fallout from the various American led invasions of Muslim countries such as Iraq in 1990-91, Afghanistan in 2001 and Iraq again from 2003 onwards to garner support from the wider Islamic world.

Seeing as many of those who identify as Muslim Australians already don't connect with Australian nationalism on the one hand, and continue to show empathy and compassion towards both the real and imaginary suffering of their fellow Muslims worldwide on the other, with many Westernised Muslims the message inherent within the Inspire and Dabiq magazines resonated well.

American Sniper is an interesting movie for many reasons. It is interesting in the first instance because it documents a reality we don't really get to hear about on mainstream media. That American citizen from Texas, Chris Kyle was an ordinary young man, apparently not even immensely patriotic, at the time when he saw those passenger planes on television smash into the World Trade Centre buildings in New York on 11th September, 2001.

That day, Chris Kyle concluded that his people, those 300 million plus Americans, their culture, values, freedoms and civilisation were under attack by a bunch of hate mongering barbarians from the Middle East. He felt he needed to do something about it. So he decided, due to this single event, to enlist in the US Marines.

Chris Kyle would eventually end up being deployed to Iraq where he became an American sniper, hence the title of the movie. Given the nature of war, in Kyle's time while serving his country he executed many people, both combatants as well as civilians. This has been acknowledged in his book and adequately portrayed in the movie.

Nobody would look at Chris Kyle and assume that he was 'radicalised' after watching the events of 11th September, and rightly so. He was a man who felt his people were under attack and he had to set the record straight and he went and enlisted in his country's army to vent his frustration.

Terrorism is the deliberate use of violence against either innocent civilians or combatants to advance political goals that go against any established order at any given time. Terrorism never has been and never will be justifiable for anyone who understands morality. Yet in order to defeat it, we must understand it for what it is.

This is where it becomes important to note that when those who identify as Muslim Australians read about such exaggerated accounts of the suffering of their fellow Muslims published by Inspire and Dabiq magazines, they are told that too many innocent Muslim civilians have been killed following the American invasions of Afghanistan and Iraq.

These people, otherwise completely detached from whatever's happening in Afghanistan or Iraq, then succumb to their extended sympathies. They have a 'Chris Kyle moment' in reverse and start to presume that their people ie. the global 'ummah' of Muslims is under attack by evil forces of the "Crusaders" that is the American-led Western world. That was the term Osama Bin Laden used to use to refer to the American government. Now it has caught on and become quite popular among many Muslims angry at the West.

Since Islam is only a religion and not a country, there is no official military to enlist in like Chris Kyle could, in order to defend his people. Aggrieved Muslims end up leaving their otherwise good, democratic, and free lives in Australia to travel to some war torn country where there is an attempt underway to create that global caliphate, hence, the staggering number of Muslim Australians like Muhammad Elomar and Dr Tareq Kamleh who responded to the call.

So it isn't wrong to say that when Muslim Australians get radicalised, that is only an extreme manifestation of their extended sympathies. No one would disagree that if some Australian regardless of their faith wanted to, on humanitarian grounds, offer support and sympathy towards the suffering of another group of humans somewhere around the world in a non-violent way that would be perfectly normal.

Plenty of Australians, Americans, Brits and other Westerners donate generously for instance to orphans in Ethiopia with whom they have absolutely no personal, cultural or ancestral, let alone religious, connection. This is in fact a form of extended sympathy, but not one anyone would have any issues with.

It is when these extended sympathies start to stretch out to a point where, based on a false and exaggerated narrative perpetuated by terrorist organisations, Muslim Australians feel compelled to vent their anger on innocent civilians or combatants alike, that is when we know that things have gone too far.

It still remains interesting to wonder why it is that Muslims struggle to reconcile their extended sympathies and loyalty towards Islam and other Muslims with their current Australian national identities? Perhaps looking at the way Jewish Americans, Jewish Australians and Jewish Brits have integrated themselves into the mainstream fabric of American, Australian and British societies is the role model Muslims need to follow.

Is assimilation the answer?

Migration is an interesting phenomenon for many reasons. Firstly, it is somewhat unnatural because migration as we understand in the modern West, really only happens in the modern West. What that means is, people in the developing world generally do not pack their bags and decide that they want to move to Shanghai or Timbuktu to start a new life. They would normally go to London or New York and other parts of the West, of which Australia is a part.

This form of migration is relatively recent phenomenon that began in the years after the end of World War II. Why? Because the war years from 1937 to 1945 had caused a lot of damage to cities in the Western world that had participated in the war and cost immense number of lives, mostly males that were fighting through conscription on the front lines. There was an emergent shortage of labour and many politicians at the time thought it might be a good idea, for Western countries, to open their doors up to migration from developing countries.

Although this wasn't the only reason. Of course, the other reason was that many politicians in the West felt morally obliged to accept the large influx of refugees created by World War II. These two factors combined eventually led to the dismantling of previous restrictions on immigration across the Western world and especially so in the English speaking world.

Like the United States and Canada, Australia too had an *Immigration Restriction Act (1901)* which has since come to be known as the 'White Australia Policy'.[124] While migrants and refugees from non-European backgrounds continued to come to Australia even during the heyday of the policy, the criteria for entry was much tougher.

As decades went on, due to international pressures Australia relaxed its migration policies and began to accept large numbers of migrants from many different parts of the world. The original migrants to Australia after World War II were the Italians, Greeks and Jews. Given our involvement in the Vietnam War, we took in plenty of Vietnamese in the 1970s and 1980s. The Lebanese and other varieties of Arab and Muslim minorities have come to Australia during different stages.

The question of 'assimilation' and 'integration' never seems to escape the public discussion whenever migration is mentioned, especially among right wingers. There are several reasons for this. First up, there is a view on the part of some, that migrants do not come here to blend in with our society and that they wish to make Australia more like the lands from which they came. This certainly does seem like a convenient explanation every time we drive through the streets of suburbs that seem to resemble some foreign country.

There are streets in parts of Lakemba and Auburn where you see more women walking around in the head to toe Islamic garbs than ordinarily dressed Western women. Add to that, the fact that today almost every Australian capital city has a Chinatown. Although it is interesting that nobody complains about those Chinatowns. If anything, people seem to have this appreciation for the fact that they're able to get noodles and peking duck at some ungodly hour of the night for a relatively cheap price right here at home without the need to jump on a plane to China.

The same isn't true of Lakemba. The only conclusion to draw from that is that Australians are quite indifferent to the demographic and cosmetic shifts in their towns and suburbs, what they seem more concerned about is the associated risk they feel that is brought here due to Muslim migration. The Chinese may also be stacking out your suburbs, selling Chinese food, dressing like Chinese people but nobody identifies them as a threat.

The case with Muslims and other varieties of Arabs was once like that, but since September 11 things have not been so good. So while we can acknowledge it's important to discuss assimilation and integration, it is equally important to remember that these terms are harder to define than we realise at first sight.

For starters, I dislike using the term 'assimilation' because that's what the Nazis tried to do to the Jews early up during Hitler's reign. They tried to force the Jews to dress and act like ordinary Germans and to 'assimilate' into German culture and society. This meant that Jewish men could no longer grow beards, or grow their sideburns which is a religious requirement in the Torah called 'payot' and their women could no longer wear the headscarf, their male children could no longer be circumcised, they could no longer build Synagogues in German towns nor speak or write Yiddish on Jewish shops, nor be able to sell Kosher meat.

That was what assimilation meant when the term was originally used. It was a horrible thing to force a minority to erase every trace of its heritage culture and to force them to act like something else. What skin is it off anybody's nose how somebody chooses to dress so long as they're not forcing you to dress that way? I do agree that the face veil otherwise known as the Niqab or head to toe Burqa isn't even compulsory in Islam, nor do large numbers of Muslim women in Australia wear them.

And to be perfectly honest, neither the Niqab nor the Burqa has any place in modern Australian society. People at the very least, reserve the right to see our faces when we walk around in public. Other than this, I have no issue with the headscarf seeing as plenty of Orthodox Jewish women, Catholic Nuns, Hindu and Sikh women also choose to dress that way and not just Muslims.

Given that assimilation was a term that carried some negative implications due to the context of World War II, the term 'integration' is preferred. What is meant by that is if you choose to migrate to another country, then you have an obligation to respect the local laws, customs, culture and language, and you pledge your loyalty to your new home. That to me is a fairly moderate stance which expects the least little bit from a migrant. No, we are not like the Nazi Germans and we do not want to force migrants to erase every trace of their heritage.

What we want to encourage them to do is to find the right balance as I have written in previous sections. To those who only know me through reading this book, or by seeing me on television, or by following my page on Facebook, I might seem completely Australian on the inside and outside. That is only half the story. I speak fluent Arabic in a Levantine dialect spoken in Lebanon, Syria, Jordan, Israel and the Palestinian territories.

I not only enjoy eating Levantine Arabic cuisine, I am also an exceptionally good cook thanks to my mother passing down her secret recipes. As I say, there is nothing wrong with preserving one's heritage language and cuisine. If done right, this can compliment the Australian identity rather than act as a competitor towards it. The loyalty should be to Australia and Australia alone. When you live in Australia, send your kids to school in Australia, are educated at Australian TAFE and universities, pay your taxes to Australia and receive Medicare benefits from the Australian government among tonnes of other benefits, then it is perfectly reasonable for Australia to expect that you would at least be loyal to its national interests. This level of integration isn't at odds with Islamic teachings. It's not even that Muslims can integrate into the West, it's more so that they're obliged to do so by Islam. When we look back at Islamic history, we find that wherever Islam spread it actually appropriated local customs and cultures into its own, created culinary and linguistic hybrids and Islamic governments employed local representatives in high ranking positions.

Integration is not only possible under Islam - it is highly encouraged. There is historical evidence to prove this point. Look at the manner in which Islam spread in Egypt, Persia, the Byzantine Empire, China and India. Muslims didn't entirely impose their culture upon the subjugated peoples.

Instead, they gradually appropriated local customs and traditions creating cultural synthesis, hybrid languages and allowed for assimilation to occur organically. Muslim rulers took on locals as their advisers and rulers, both shared with each other what they knew of the world and together created the perfect assimilated mix. When understood correctly, Sharia law instructs Muslims to obey the law of the land in which they reside. This is not an instruction that comes straight from the Quran. Rather it comes from carefully crafted jurisprudential rulings based on the principles of the Quran and Prophet Muhammad's traditions.

Non-Muslim countries in which Muslim citizens are guaranteed fundamental rights, including the freedom to practice their religion without fear or prejudice, are classified in Islam as Dar al-Aman or 'The Abode of Safety' as per the rulings of renowned jurist, Imam Al-Sarakhsi.

As virtually every Western country to which Muslims generally migrate gives them the freedom to practice their religion, there is no obligation on any Muslim to pick up arms and rebel against that nation's interests. There is no reason for any Muslim to enforce his or her ways on to the host community either. If anything, the Muslim has a religious obligation to do what he and she can to integrate themselves into the host society and be loyal citizens.

As we have discussed at length through various parts of this book, it is the present-day Muslim's political mindset and narrow outlook on world affairs that gets in the way of them being able to express loyalty towards the West. The fact that I can be both Muslim and loyal to Australia at the same time shows that it isn't impossible to do and that they are not mutually exclusive. The Jewish people have done it for centuries and Muslims can do the same. I am hoping that this book will inspire many to do just that.

Racism and Islamophobia: Are they actually real?

The words "racism" and "Islamophobia" are thrown around so often whenever someone tries to criticise anything to do with Muslims, some of us have genuinely begun to wonder whether our society might be racist or Islamophobic. Of course, in actual fact, we are neither.

This is an unusual question to even be thinking about to say the least, because the mere fact that we can debate such things while tolerating a diversity of opinions on the matter is itself proof to the contrary. Nobody would debate whether Australian society has a natural bias or prejudice against Eskimos or Tibetans because we don't have many Eskimos and Tibetans here and they don't feature in news headlines. Even if some did exist in this place, they're probably living quietly in their own corner, we don't hear about them. The fact that our media, our politicians and general public finds itself debating whether or not we are Islamophobic bears proof that we have let many Muslims in to this country in the first place - a nation not otherwise founded by Islam or Muslims.

The proof is in the pudding, if Australia was racist or Islamophobic, it wouldn't have opened its doors to Muslim immigration. It is that simple. Muslims wouldn't have had the chance to come and live here, let alone complain that Australians were racist and Islamophobic. We often forget that immigration is not a natural phenomenon. Those who advocate for multiculturalism and mass immigration often make it sound like humans have always moved around from place to place in search of a better life and go on to suggesting that the same should apply today. This simply isn't true. For most of the human history, people have tended to stick closely with their village, religious community or language group. This is the key reason why we have nation-states on the world map: France for the French, Israel for the Jews, the 22 Arab countries for Arabs and Japan for the Japanese. While there can be some level of cultural or limited ethnic diversity within nation-states, there is always a dominant cultural and ethnic character and most citizens feel comfortable enough sticking within that. This doesn't make you racist; it's natural human behaviour to prefer to stick with your own kind.

What's highly unusual is that in the Western world, especially in the English-speaking nations of Britain, Canada, United States,

Australia and New Zealand, we don't operate this way. These countries have tended to subscribe to a form of civic nationalism as opposed to the universal norm of ethnic nationalism. While each of these countries was set up by Anglo-Celts of European ancestry, it's almost considered a sin these days for an American or Aussie to say they wish to maintain their Anglo-Celtic European majority in their countries.

Nobody would bat an eyelid if someone in Japan, China or India said they wanted their nations to maintain their Japanese, Chinese or Indian cultural or ethnic character. For whatever reason, the countries of the West and especially the English-speaking nations are held to a different standard. The mere fact that these are the nations that have gone out of their ways to welcome new migrants since the end of World War II, resettled millions of refugees in their midst, given them the same voting rights in their elections and even passed anti-discrimination laws in their Parliaments to give minorities special protection is itself proof that these countries are not racist.

In Australia, we have Section 116 of the Constitution that guarantees religious freedom. In addition, we have the Racial Discrimination Act (1975) which is a legal tool designed to fight racism in this country. Most countries outside of the English-speaking West don't even allow migration and the acquisition of citizenship through a process of naturalisation, let alone enact legislation to protect the rights of minorities and migrants. We're the only ones who do that, yet oddly we're the ones that are frequently the subject of global criticism and accusations of racism and Islamophobia.

Muslims have been coming to Australia since the mid to late 1800s as cameleers and carpet merchants from Afghanistan. Even during the decades of the 'White Australia Policy' Australia was welcoming Muslim migrants. My own family is a classic example of this. What we should never forget is that nobody puts a gun to anyone's head and forces them to migrate to a Western nation. People make that choice voluntarily. Muslims choose to call Australia home, as they do with other nations of the English-speaking world.

It's safe to conclude that life must be better in those countries than the conditions Muslims leave behind in their countries of origin. If this wasn't the case, it would defy logic to bother moving here. In as long as Muslims have been on Australian soil, sadly there have been tensions despite the fact that this country has bent over backwards to make them feel welcome, in ways other countries never would. It's a little known fact, but Australia's first Muslim terrorist incident actually took place in 1915 when two Afghan ice cream vendors Badshah Mohammed Gul and Mullah Abdullah opened fire at a train full of civilians at Broken Hill, New South Wales killing 6 injuring 7.[125] When investigated they said they launched the attack as a protest against Australia's involvement in World War I fighting the Ottoman Empire. This theme sounds eerily familiar. When Man Haron Monis attacked Lindt Cafe during the Sydney Siege in December 2014, he too had expressed his discontent at Australia's involvement in the wars in Afghanistan and Iraq.[126]

It is deeply troubling that more than a century later, Muslim fanaticism has not evolved. We continue to have groups of people living in the West, benefiting from the opportunities and freedoms available to them, while conjuring up grievances in their minds over stuff that happens abroad and their loyalties have tended to lie elsewhere. It is far more important to ask whether it is possible for Muslims to be loyal to the West than wondering whether or not we are racist or Islamophobic, and that will be the subject of the next section.

It must be noted that racism is the belief about the superiority of one's own race and the ability to discriminate against others based on that belief. By this definition, Adolf Hitler who believed that the Aryan race was superior to Jews, gypsies and everyone else was certainly racist. But modern Australia is far from it. As this section has demonstrated, in this country we not only have a long history of welcoming migrants from different parts of the world, we even go out of our way to enact legislation that guarantees them their religious freedoms and protects them from any form of discrimination.

It's no surprise that Muslims have not only been able to come and call Australia home, they have operated halal businesses, run government funded Islamic schools and featured strongly in public life in this country. There are Muslims like Bachar Houli who played top level AFL for Richmond, Usman Khawaja who plays test cricket for Australia, journalist and TV host Waleed Aly, Federal Member of Parliament for the seat of Cowan Dr Anne Aly, Senator for New South Wales Dr Mehreen Faruqi and Ahmed Fahour the former CEO of Australia Post. All prominent success stories of Muslim Australians in their own rights. Clearly, there is absolutely no institutional racism and Islamophobia in this country and those who constantly complain about such things are generally either looking too much into things that often have simpler explanations or experiencing things that don't represent broader Australian society.

It must be born in mind that Australians are on average a sensible people and this isn't even a new phenomenon. Five decades ago, we as a nation were asked whether or not to extend the right to vote to Indigenous Australians and more than 90% of the voting public said yes.[127] Only last year, two thirds of Australians voted to legalise same sex marriage.[128] This shows that Australians do not like to discriminate.

If Australians were inherently racist, then you would think that one could potentially start a movement or a political party calling for a ban on Hindu, Sikh, Buddhist or any other kind of immigration. Such a thing hasn't happened and if it did, it is guaranteed to be a flop. This is because there is no inherent fear, paranoia or suspicion about Indians or Hindus, Sikhs and Buddhists in general in Australian society.

Yet there are politicians within Australia's mainstream political parties as well as many fringe parties that have expressed concerns about Islam and Muslim immigration. George Christensen from the Liberal National Party in Queensland, Liberal-turned-Australian Conservative Senator for South Australia Cory Bernardi, Liberal Senator for Tasmania Eric Abetz and Senator Fraser Anning are all examples of relatively mainstream Australian politicians that have taken a hardline stance against Muslim immigration.

Add to this, the rise of fringe political parties that run on a populist anti-Muslim platform such as the Australian Liberty Alliance, Rise Up Australia and Pauline Hanson's One Nation. These parties generally do manage to receive a significant chunk of the popular vote. Half a million Australians voted for One Nation at the 2016 Federal Election.[129] Why is it that so many Australians are concerned enough about Muslims to be able to vote for anti-Muslim politicians and political parties?

Answering this question has been the central theme of this book and it should be clear enough by this stage that, due to factors laid out in previous chapters, the rise in Muslim terrorist incidents has not helped Australians form a particularly favourable view of Muslims nor of their religion. It is true that many of the politicians, journalists and members of the public that are sceptical of Islam aren't always well qualified on the subject to express a sophisticated opinion. In their defence, most Australians hardly know much about Australian history or Christianity for that matter, which is supposed to be the foundation of our own society, how could we expect them to go out of their ways to educate themselves about Islam. People all over the world arrive at the simplest conclusion they can, regardless of whether those conclusions are right or wrong.

Muslims are no different. When America invaded Iraq, Muslims assumed Americans hate Muslims and wished to erase Islam off the world map. Nobody stopped to realise that Saddam Hussein was hardly a practising Muslim himself. He drank alcohol and subscribed to Ba'athism which is a form of nationalist Arab socialism that goes completely against Islam. He was a brutal dictator. Yet if Americans topple Saddam, Muslims view him as a representative of Islam and the Americans as evil "Crusaders". So, it isn't exactly fair if we forgive Muslims for their oversimplified views on the West and began picking on Australians for their oversimplified views on Islam. The truth is that anyone and everyone can have oversimplified views on their day and in this case, the idea that Australian society is racist or Islamophobic is far from true. Australians since September 11 have been skeptical of Islam and suspicious of Muslims on occasion, but overall, most people are still fairly respectful towards Muslims despite the perceived threat of terrorism.

Before anyone thinks that Australians are racist or Islamophobic, remember that we are talking about a country where a sitting Prime Minister invites the leaders of its Muslim community to his house for iftar dinners in Ramadan as Malcolm Turnbull did in June 2016.[130] It is interesting to note that among the list of attendees were Waleed Aly who is a well-known critic of that Prime Minister's own Party and his convert Muslim wife Dr Susan Carland, social activist Yassmin Abdel Magied and the notorious Sheikh Shady who is on the record making controversial remarks about gays and lesbians.[131] If this isn't a tolerant society free from Islamophobia, then I'm not sure what is.

The Saudi Government does not let non-Muslims enter the city of Mecca, not even for tourism purposes.[132] We hardly hear any criticism directed at them for their hardline entry laws. All the criticism seems to be directed at the English-speaking West where ironically there is far greater freedom of movement for people. This sort of hypocrisy and double standards should not be tolerated in any shape or form. Australia is neither racist nor Islamophobic and people should stop using these exaggerated excuses to misrepresent our country.

Can Muslims be loyal to the West?

The question of loyalty is important. I would say, it's especially important in the age of mass immigration where so many people have chosen to call a Western nation home of their own free will. The least we can expect is for them to be loyal to the country that has taken them in and enabled them to have a fair go in life. But we must approach this topic of loyalty with some care and proper nuance. As much as loyalty is important, it must first be defined. What do we even mean when we say 'loyalty'?

If an Englishman living in Australia after 30 years continues to support England in the Ashes against Australia, is he being disloyal? I guess what it comes down to in the end is political loyalty, not any other form of loyalty. There are plenty of Australians who support Manchester United in soccer and when Man U plays against an Australian club, they will still support Man U over that Australian club. This does not mean that those Australians are less patriotic, let alone disloyal, to their country, it simply means that they choose to support a soccer club that happens to be based in England as opposed to a local one.

Supporting Man U does not in any shape or form compromise the national interests, security or integrity of the Commonwealth of Australia. It does not amount to sedition in any shape or form. However, if an Englishman working for the Australian government was made privy to sensitive confidential information and if he were to pass that on to the British government then surely, he has been disloyal.

So, what it really comes down to is whether or not you are politically loyal towards the nation-state in which you happen to hold your citizenship. The kind of loyalty we are seeking from citizens, migrant or otherwise but especially migrants, is a kind of political loyalty. People ought not pursue acts that can compromise the security, integrity and national interests.

Therefore I have never been comfortable with the idea of dual nationality. It is true that once you have another passport, it may well bring some benefits such as being able to travel freely to certain countries. The European Union passport certainly springs to mind as an example and many Greek, Italian or French Australians quite enjoy the fact that they hold both an Australian and an EU passport because that enables them to literally drive around Europe as if it was one giant borderless country, no visas required.

This is all great, and nobody would argue against it. But imagine if a French Australian was concurrently being paid by the French government to act as a spy and gather intelligence on our military capacity for argument's sake, which would most certainly be an act of espionage and disloyalty.

Over the centuries, the Jews were harassed in Europe over the question of loyalty. They were frequently accused of putting their own community and its needs above those of the kingdom or nation within which they resided. This level of pressure often amounted to rampant antisemitism. One has to bear in mind that loyalty to a country or nation isn't an absolute. No one can expect another citizen to abandon all forms of associations with foreign entities.

Remember that each of us on a day to day basis buys foreign products, avails foreign services, makes businesses with foreign partners, sends our children to study in foreign colleges and universities, and benefits from selling products and services to foreign buyers. At the end of the day, we live in a global community where each of us will engage with the party that serves our best interests regardless of which geographical boundary that party happens to be in.

With all that said, it nonetheless remains perfectly reasonable to expect that no action or transaction in which citizens engage must bring disrepute upon the interests of our own nation. Whether we are talking about Muslim Australians or non-Muslim Australians, each of us has an obligation to do our level best to abide by the rules of this country. The recent Section 44 related crises that was triggered by former Greens Senators Scott Ludlam and Larissa Waters which also ended up causing a by-election in the then Deputy Prime Minister Barnaby Joyce's seat of New England was a telling experience.

It was a real wake up call for Australians to start re-thinking questions of national loyalty. When it comes to Muslim communities, the question of loyalty becomes a tricky one. There are certain things a Muslim is religiously forbidden from doing such as drinking alcohol or eating pork. So if a Muslim Australian happens to avoid going out partying, drinking and having a pork sausage, someone could easily turn around and accuse that person of not 'fitting in' or 'acting normal' or perhaps even showing subtle disloyalty to the mainstream culture of this country.

But ask yourself, does that really make the person disloyal if they choose to live by a certain dietary code? No. Remember that the Jewish people have followed the kosher dietary code which is almost identical to the halal dietary code. The point being that, the food you eat, the way you dress so long as your face is visible, the area you reside in all come down to personal choice and it is not reasonable of any of us to expect someone from a different cultural background to go out of their way to do things we expect them to do just to prove how Australian they are.

After all, there are countless Anglo-Celtic Australians of European ancestry who choose not to drink alcohol, hence we have the word teetotallers in English. Mormons are a perfect example of this. Many Australians concerned about global warming, pollution, excess population and animal cruelty tend to turn towards veganism as a dietary alternative. They too wouldn't say "cheers!" to a pint of beer or that pork sausage, yet they could be 7th generation descendants of ancestors on the First Fleet in 1788. Does this make those people less Australian? No. Does this amount to disloyalty? No.

At the end of the day we are a free nation, with a free culture, and we minimise the extent to which we interfere in each other's lives as much as possible. This in fact is what makes us different from other countries like Saudi Arabia, Iran and Afghanistan, where the way you dress, the food you eat, from whom you buy your meat are all often dictated by the state, or your local community leader or a head of the family. We are not a culture of control freaks.

Yet who would deny that each of us has an indispensable responsibility to protect, preserve and advance our national interests in the political sense. Supporting a foreign soccer team may be tolerated but supporting a foreign power in an act of war against Australia is intolerable. Practising elements of your religious beliefs and culture are tolerable but attempting to override the norms and culture of this country are not tolerable.

Muslim loyalty to the West is an important question to ask in the world since September 11. So many Muslim terrorist attacks have taken place and they're always motivated by some Muslim extremist feeling sympathies for the perceived or actual suffering of the fellow members of his 'ummah' somewhere overseas. In fact, you don't even need to be a Muslim extremist to feel the pain of other Muslims, you only need to be a Muslim full stop. Lots of mainstream Muslims, like various other communities have their extended sympathies as discussed earlier.

So is it possible to be a Muslim and be loyal to the West? The answer to this question might well surprise you. Not only is it possible, it is in fact highly encouraged in Islam. Muslims are required to obey the law of the land in which they reside. When Prophet Muhammad was originally facing persecution at the hands of his own Quraish tribe, the ruling elite in Mecca, he instructed a group of his disciples to seek refuge in the neighbouring Christian Kingdom of Abyssinia and to abide by their laws and respect local customs while there.[133]

Of course, Muslims can maintain their core beliefs and teachings while living in the West, the same way Jews, Hindus, Sikhs and other religious minorities do so long as they're not shoving their practices down other people's throats. That Section 116 of the Constitution which we have spoken about previously prohibits the Commonwealth from legislating on or preventing the free exercise of any religion.[134] So a Muslim isn't being disloyal to the West by merely practising his religion, but if anyone engages in an act of espionage, or incites to violence against the state, then that is most certainly an act of disloyalty and it should be dealt with through the full force of the law.

In America there are plenty of Jews who are proudly Jewish as well as proudly American. The thought of having to pick one over the other neither occurs to most people nor does it need to. One must be mature and keep a balance between their religious beliefs and civic duties. There is no reason why Muslims could not be proud Australians while being good Muslims at the same time.

Australia, We Have a Solution

Everyone has a story: you, me, your next-door neighbour... all of us. You've just read mine and in so doing, many of your common assumptions, fears, suspicions, criticisms, misperceptions and concerns about my religion were challenged, debunked, disproven or possibly reinforced. Whatever the case, we agree on one fundamental issue, that is, all of the violence, bloodshed and murder being committed in the name of Islam must cease immediately.

We agree that women should be treated with dignity and respect. By now, you know that they are but, as with other societies, Muslims are not perfect. Just as Julia Gillard felt she was attacked for being a woman, even though you and I possibly disagree with her on that, we know that if a woman is still feeling that way then we as a society have some work to do. Like Westerners, Muslim people can be well-intentioned, warm, hospitable, kind, generous, compassionate and empathetic. Not all.

There are black sheep's in every community. Sadly, in the world since September 11, too many black sheep's have emerged in the name of a God they barely understand. They have murdered endlessly, mostly their own people, and often other people, in the name of a religion they barely follow. They purport themselves to walk in the footsteps of a Prophet who, if alive today, would never approve of the things that they do.

The idea that Islam may yet desire for its right to exercise a free jurisdiction where Muslims may live and practice their religion freely is no secret by this stage. A caliphate if you will, but the caliphate it demands was a caliphate of the hearts and minds, not a caliphate of guns and violence. Many caliphates existed throughout history, as we saw throughout this book. From the Umayyads through the Ottomans and the Mughals, these caliphates produced some of the greatest literary works of science, maths, alchemy and poetry the world has yet seen.

A caliphate of the hearts and minds is not different from a Vatican City that has no authority to wage war. People don't care that there exists a Catholic theocracy somewhere on this planet, landlocked within Rome in Italy. A caliphate of the hearts and minds would be the utopia where Muslim women, men, children, the old, gays, lesbians, blacks and whites live together side by side in peace and harmony.

That was the vision of the Prophet Muhammad. He was not a man who attempted to wage war for war's sake. He sent his people to make hijrah, i.e. migrate and seek refuge in peace in Abyssinia. He was a man who was signing peace treaties in an era that knew nothing about peace treaties. He gave women the respect they lacked in other cultures where, like Helen of Troy and Cleopatra, they were seen as sexually corrupt.

He was a man who preached that wars should be a measure of last resort. That in defensive war, no trees should be cut down, no fields should set alight, no women or children must be harmed, no elderly should be killed, no personal revenge should be sought and prisoners of war must be treated with dignity and respect. It was the precise result of these tolerant teachings that Islam protected its religious minorities. The example of Islamic tolerance remains widespread to date, from the Coptic Christians of Alexandria through to the Mizrahi Jews of Yemen.

By their fruits you shall know them, said Jesus. So too should Prophet Muhammad be judged by the fruits he brought to the world. Through his teachings, the Islamic world has become a bastion in producing some of the finest female leaders and warriors, like Umm Ammarah to Benazir Bhutto.

Still, we have a problem. The problem is not what you thought it was before reading this book, I should hope. But there still is a problem. Too many Muslims have deviated from the beautiful and respectful teachings of authentic Islam as taught to me by my parents and elders, indeed as intended by the founder of this great religion, Prophet Muhammad. For as long as these Muslims remain deviant on their own paths, the world will continue to form extreme judgements.

This is not the fault of the critic who gets suspicious about Islam and Muslims, it is in fact the fault of the Muslim for giving the opportunity to be misjudged. The Western world is far from perfect and that's no secret. We have often waged wars where peace would have sufficed. We have often generalised and judged entire groups of people for the actions of the very few. But for all our flaws, we remain a decent and free society that is the envy of the world.

Islam may be great, but Islamic civilisation (as in the art, literature, architecture, poetry and collection of societies inspired by Islam) is no longer so great. Instead of moving forwards from the days of

Abu Nuwas and those gay caliphs, we have tended to go backwards. That's nobody else's fault but ours, as Muslims.

Remember when the French had a crisis; there was a French revolution in 1789. Remember when the Americans were hard done by the British Empire; George Washington led a revolution against England's King George III and eventually succeeded in putting the first modern democracy on the world's map. No foreign aid or external power came to the rescue of the French and the American people.

The Quran preaches that God helps those who help themselves. It's time those Muslims who know their religion in its pure and authentic form start putting these words into practice. It's time they call out the extremists and cleanse them from within their society. Jewish fundamentalist Yigal Amir assassinated Israeli Prime Minister Yitzhak Rabin in 1995 for his support of a Palestinian state under the Oslo Accords. You would never meet a Jew that makes up excuses for the actions of Yigal Amir. That is where Muslims need to be.

In the aftermath of terrorist attacks, we too often see Muslim community leaders, secular and religious ones, going on the front foot and antagonising the governments of the Western world where those terrorist attacks often take place. This isn't necessarily because mainstream Muslims agree with everything the terrorist does, but rather because they falsely assume that the government has a hidden agenda against them.

It defies all logic to think that Western governments would seek to pick on a relatively helpless religious minority. There is nothing to gain out of doing that. Western governments have to spend billions of dollars each year on counterterrorism, intelligence gathering and law enforcement just to keep their citizens safe. Yet if an incident manages to occur, the public in Western democracies can be very harsh in punishing its governments. The public sees such attacks as intelligence failures on the government's part and that ends up building ill will which, in the worst-case scenario, could cost a government an election.

No Western government on purpose wants to see Muslims be demonised, dehumanised, marginalised or interrogated about terrorism for the sake of it. They have a job to do and that requires keeping our civilians safe. This includes Muslims too. Many Muslims in the West have been victims of terrorism.

If a government must use some degree of profiling to search for explosives on board passenger jets, Muslims should not feel that this is the result of some sinister Islamophobic agenda against them. Imagine if a Muslim son dies in a terrorist attack launched by another Muslim, the first thing his parents would do is blame the airport security for not going harder on catching potential terrorists.

These points sound so unbelievably basic that you would think most people would be able to figure all this out for themselves. Sadly, with this whole topic of Islam and terrorism, emotions run deep and often end up clouding people's ability to make sense of what is going on.

So many Muslims who would frequently dismiss Western culture and society as materialistic, hedonistic, lacking spirituality and family values would, in the same breath, refuse to go back and live in their own countries. This is not Islamic behaviour. Whenever the Prophet encouraged his followers to seek a new life in non-Muslim territory, he encouraged them to respect the laws of their adopted land and be decent towards its citizens.

If ever there has been a time for Muslims to start putting into practice these beautiful teachings of their Prophet, it is today. Instead of being immersed in a perpetual state of victimhood, Muslims must take responsibility for their own actions. It is not constructive to blame America, Israel and the rest of their Western allies for all the faults and failures of Muslim societies.

What's even more embarrassing is that on the one hand, there is the blame game that is culturally ingrained within the Muslim psyche where America is seen as the 'Great Satan' yet on the other hand, the same America-hating Muslims would literally kill or die to have a US Green Card so they can start a new life in America.

This is a cognitive dissonance that only Muslims can come to terms within their own times. Is America a force of good or a force of evil? Make up your mind and stick with your conclusions once you have. It is hypocritical to seek death and destruction upon a country while wanting to reap the benefits of the freedom and opportunity it offers.

Lack of assimilation into Western society isn't the issue as we have seen from the examples of perfectly assimilated Westernised jihadis like Dr Tarek Kamleh. Lack of loyalty towards the West most certainly is part of the problem and only Muslims can fix that by looking inward.

These problems are complex and they will not go away overnight. If we're serious about achieving harmony in society, we must take the time to understand the complexity and nuance of these issues. Muslims and non-Muslims need to understand each other's perspectives not in the words of our critics, but in our own words. To that end, I sincerely hope this book is a humble step in the right direction. I hope you enjoyed reading it and I hope you will help spread its message.

NOTES

1. Peter Wood, "Love and Hate in the Library", *The East Hampton Star*, April 25th, 2019. (online).
2. "Quran - 51:56", Quran.com. (online).
3. Esposito, J. L. (2000). *The Oxford History of Islam*. Oxford University Press: p.78
4. Holt, P. M., Lambton, A. K., & Lewis, B. (1970). *The Cambridge history of Islam*. University Press: p.540
5. Sekulow, J. (2017). *Unholy Alliance: The Agenda Iran, Russia, and Jihadists share for Conquering the World*. Simon & Schuster: p.81
6. Gil, M. (2011). *Jews in Islamic Countries in the Middle Ages*. Brill: p.21
7. "The Print Revolution", Columbia Law School. (online).
8. Rob S. Harvey, "Protestant Reformation", The First Amendment Encyclopedia. (online).
9. "Treaty of Westphalia", The Avalon Project (Yale Law School), 2008. (online).
10. "Declaration of Independence, July 4, 1776", The Avalon Project (Yale Law School), 2008. (online).
11. Esposito, J. L. (2000). *The Oxford history of Islam*. Oxford Univ. Press: p.624
12. Donald Deskins, Jr., Hanes Walton, Jr., and Sherman Puckett, "Presidential Elections, 1789-2008", University of Michigan Press, 2008. (online).
13. Oona A. Hathaway, Scott J. Shapiro, "Outlawing War? It Actually Worked", *The New York Times*, September 2, 2017. (online).
14. J.B. Bury, "History of the Later Roman Empire", The University of Chicago, 1923. (online).
15. Connor Potts, "King Henry VIII", Duke University, 2020. (online).
16. Fulcher of Chartres, "Urban II: Speech at Council of Clermont", Fordham University, 1996. (online).
17. "Galileo Galilei", Utah State University. (online).
18. Mattson, I., Nesbitt-Larking, P., & Tahir, N. (2015). *Religion and representation: Islam and democracy*. Cambridge Scholars Publishing: p.292
19. Cooper, A. S. (2018). *Fall of Heaven: The Pahlavis and the final days of Imperial Iran*. Picador: p.38
20. Duri, A. A. (2012). *The Historical Formation of the Arab Nation* (RLE: The Arab Nation). Routledge: p.39
21. Al-Rasheed, M., Kersten, C., & Shterin, M. (2015). *Demystifying the Caliphate: Historical memory and contemporary contexts*. Oxford University Press: p.23
22. "The Egyptian Muslim Brotherhood", *Religious Literacy Project* (Harvard Divinity School). (online).
23. Islam, M. N. (1989). *Pakistan and Malaysia: A comparative study in national integration*. Sterling Pub: p.130

24 Abbas, S. B. (2014). *Pakistan's blasphemy laws from Islamic empires to the Taliban.* University of Texas Press: p.75
25 Bowen, W. H. (2015). *The History of Saudi Arabia, 2nd ed.* ABC-CLIO, LLC: p.13
26 "88 Australians Killed in Bomb Attacks in Bali", Australian Broadcasting Corporation, 2002. (online).
27 Gabriel Samuels, "Sadiq Khan: London mayor says being prepared for terror attacks 'part and parcel' of living in a major city", *The Independent,* May 25, 2017. (online).
28 "Death Penalty Fast Facts", Cable News Network, August 4, 2020. (online).
29 Cook, S. A. (2013). *Laws of Moses and the code of Hammurabi.* Gaunt: p.272
30 "Crime & Punishment", Medieval Chronicles, 2014. (online).
31 "How many witnesses are required to prove adultery?", Islam StackExchange, July 12, 2012. (online).
32 "Witness", Jewish Virtual Library, 2008. (online).
33 "Muslim scholar's fatwa condemns terrorism", Cable News Network, March 4, 2010. (online).
34 "Fatwas, rulings and authoritative statements against terrorism in Islam", Faculty of Arts (The University of Melbourne), 2019. (online).
35 "58 Bible Verses about Right Hand Of God", Knowing-Jesus.com. (online).
36 Jon Bloom, "God Rested on the Seventh Day", *Desiring God,* March 26, 2016. (online).
37 "Four horsemen of the apocalypse", *Encyclopædia Britannica,* August 26, 2020. (online).
38 "Crossing the Red Sea - Bible Story", Bible Study Tools, March 1, 2018. (online).
39 "Jesus Turns Water into Wine Bible Story", Bible Study Tools, October 20, 2017. (online).
40 "Burāq: Islamic legend", *Encyclopædia Britannica,* July 20, 1998. (online).
41 Dominic Casciani, "Who is Anjem Choudary and why was he in prison?", British Broadcasting Corporation, October 19, 2018. (online).
42 Ben Sales, "Exploring Ties Between Halacha and Shariah", Forward.com, November 2, 2011. (online).
43 "Bakham Bashi", *Encyclopaedia Judaica* (Encyclopedia.com), August 12, 2020. (online).
44 Sue Reid, "As Islamic extremists declare Britain's first Sharia law zone, the worrying social and moral implications", *Daily Mail,* July 30, 2011. (online).
45 Lin Taylor, "Explainer: What is Sharia law?", Special Broadcasting Corporation, February 12, 2017. (online).
46 Peter Theodosiou, "Jihad: A word which doesn't mean war against non-Muslims", Special Broadcasting Corporation, August 28, 2016. (online).
47 Ibid.

48 Shaykh Abdool Rahman Khan, "Wanton Killing of Innocents in The Name of Islam", Islamic Circle of Northern America, November 24, 2014. (online).
49 "Deuteronomy 20", Bible Gateway, 2020. (online).
50 Ido Ben Porat, "IDF document labels Irgun, Lehi as 'terrorist organizations", Israel National News, June 8, 2017. (online).
51 "Deuteronomy 6:4", Bible Hub. (online).
52 "Quran - 112:1", Quran.com. (online).
53 Adler, E. N. (2016). *Jewish travellers in the Middle Ages: 19 firsthand accounts*. Dover, p.46-47
54 Johnston, D. M. (2011). *Religion, Terror, and Error: U.S. Foreign Policy and the Challenge of Spiritual Engagement* (Praeger Security International). Praeger, p.59
55 Phoebe Loomes, "Invasion Day 2019 rallies shifting focus and to policy, legislation as attendance numbers swell", news.com.au, January 28, 2019. (online).
56 "Q&A: Jacqui Lambie and Yassmin Abdel-Magied exchange barbs over sharia law", Australian Broadcasting Corporation, February 13, 2017. (online).
57 Ghadanfar, M. A. (2001). *Great women of Islam: Who were given the good news of paradise*. Darussalam: p.207-215
58 "Umm 'Umarah - Nusaybah bint Ka'b", Great Women of Islam. (online).
59 Ali, S. M. (2004). *The position of women in Islam: A progressive view*. State University of New York Press: p.2
60 Ibid.
61 Ibid.
62 Moosa, E., & Kenney, J. T. (2014). Islam in the Modern World. Routledge: p.128
63 Fatton, R., & Ramazani, R. K. (2004). Future of liberal democracy Thomas Jefferson and the contemporary world. Palgrave Macmillan: p.87
64 Bhutto, B. (2008). Daughter of the East: An autobiography. Pocket Books: p.34
65 Ibid.
66 John Aglionby, "Great expectations", The Guardian, July 26, 2001. (online).
67 Bennett, C. (2010). Muslim women of power: Gender, politics, and culture in Islam. Continuum: p.136
68 Ibid., p.84
69 Syjil Ashraf, "The 8 Women Who Have Led Muslim-Majority Countries", Miss Muslim, November 9th, 2016. (online).
70 Ibid.
71 Dalia G, "Meet The Nine Muslim Women Who Have Ruled Nations", Egyptian Streets, June 9, 2015. (online).
72 Ibid.
73 Jawad Anani, "Queen Rania: A great role model", The Jordan Times, June 15,

2018. (online).
74 Kristin Hunt, "Victoria and Abdul: The Friendship that Scandalized England", Smithsonian Magazine, September 20, 2017. (online).
75 Lisa Millar, "Julia Gillard says it will take 200 years before women get equal opportunities", Australian Broadcasting Corporation, April 4, 2018. (online).
76 "Riot police rescue Gillard, Abbott from protesters", Australian Broadcasting Corporation, January 26, 2012. (online).
77 "Quran - 2:256", Quran.com. (online).
78 "Map of Jewish expulsions and resettlement areas in Europe", Florida Center for Instructional Technology (University of South Florida), 1997. (online).
79 "Who are the Maronites?", British Broadcasting Service, August 6, 2007. (online).
80 "Hezbollah claims victory, PM Hariri loses a third of seats in Lebanon's parliamentary vote", France 24, May 7, 2018. (online).
81 John Burger, "Where are the oldest churches in Africa?", Aleteia, March 29, 2019. (online).
82 Robert F. Worth, "In Syrian Villages, the Language of Jesus Lives". *The New York Times*, April 22nd, 2008. (online).
83 Kim Hjelmgaard, "Iran's Jewish community is the largest in the Mideast outside Israel – and feels safe and respected", *USA Today*, September 1, 2018. (online).
84 David J Wasserstein, "So, what did the Muslims do for the Jews?". *The Jewish Chronicle*, May 24, 2012. (online).
85 *Ibid.*
86 Eli Barnavi, "The Sephardic Exodus to the Ottoman Empire", My Jewish Learning. (online).
87 "Ottoman Empire", Jewish History (Wesleyan University), 2009. (online).
88 Rebecca Ratcliffe, "FGM rates in east Africa drop from 71% to 8% in 20 years, study shows", *The Guardian*, November 7, 2018. (online).
89 "Fatwas against FGM", Stop FGM Middle East, 2014. (online).
90 Ibid.
91 Peter Theodosiou, "Islam not responsible for 'honour killings' and female genital mutilation, experts say", Special Broadcasting Corporation, August 28, 2016. (online).
92 Ibid.
93 "Quran - 2:42", Quran.com. (online).
94 Shakira Husseinm, "The Myth of the Lying Muslim: 'Taqiyya' and the Racialization of Muslim Identity", Australian Broadcasting Corporation, May 28, 2015. (online).
95 "The Declaration of Independence", ushistory.org, 1776. (online).
96 Alice Grim, "5 Queer Muslims in History", Islam and Homosexuality,

February 5, 2015. (online).
97 Shoaib Danial, "Muslims have a long history of accepting homosexuality in society", Muslims4Liberty, June 18, 2016. (online).
98 Alice Grim, "5 Queer Muslims in History", Islam and Homosexuality, February 5, 2015. (online).
99 Alice Grim, "5 Queer Muslims in History", Islam and Homosexuality, February 5, 2015. (online).
100 Shoaib Danial, "Muslims have a long history of accepting homosexuality in society", Muslims4Liberty, June 18, 2016. (online).
101 Ibid.
102 Ibid.
103 Gerli, E. M. (2017). *Medieval Iberia: An Encyclopedia*. Routledge: p.398-399
104 Bouachrine, I. (2015). *Women and Islam: Myths, apologies, and the limits of feminist critique*: p.5-22
105 Asad Hashim, "Pakistan passes landmark transgender rights law", Al Jazeera, May 10, 2018. (online).
106 Sumeyya Ilanbey, "'Completely abhorrent': Julia Banks slams former Liberal colleague Gladys Liu", **Sydney Morning Herald,** April 16, 2019. (online).
107 "Bukhari 9/92/424", Muflihun. (online).
108 Latika Bourke, "Tony Abbott backs Lateline host Emma Alberici over fiery Hizb ut-Tahrir interview", *Sydney Morning Herald*, October 9, 2014. (online).
109 "Letter to Baghdadi", Open Letter to Baghdadi, September 19, 2014. (online).
110 Sasha Ingber, "70 Muslim Clerics Issue Fatwa Against Violence And Terrorism", NPR, May 11th, 2018. (online).
111 Charles Kurzman, "Islamic Statements Against Terrorism", University of North Carolina at Chapel Hill, August 1, 2018. (online).
112 "Global Condemnations of ISIS/ISIL", Islamic Networks Group. (online).
113 Tammy Mills, "'May their organs implode': How Melbourne teen Jake Bilardi was groomed by IS", *The Age*, November 2, 2017. (online).
114 "2010-11 Flood impacts", Department of Environment (Queensland Government), January 16, 2015. (online)
115 "2009 Victorian Bushfires", Government of Victoria, April 4th, 2019. (online).
116 "Hundreds rally at Sydney Gaza protest", Special Broadcasting Corporation, May 15, 2018. (online).
117 "Supporters of Rohingya Muslims rally in Sydney", Special Broadcasting Corporation, September 7, 2017. (online).
118 Robyn Broadbent, "No future: why we need a youth policy to counter radicalisation", *The Conversation*, October 22nd, 2014. (online).
119 Ellen Whinnett, "Australian Dr Jihad Tareq Kamleh aka Abu Yousef al-Australie, killed in Syria fighting for ISIS, according to unverified reports", *The Advertiser*, June 8, 2018. (online).

120 "Ottoman Empire", History.com, November 3, 2017. (online).
121 "A Timeline of the U.S.-Led War on Terror", History.com, February 1, 2019. (online).
122 Jason Hanna, "Here's how ISIS was really founded", Cable News Network, August 13, 2016. (online).
123 Jane Ferguson, "After the fall of ISIS caliphate, its capital remains a city of the dead", Public Broadcasting Service, April 4, 2019. (online).
124 "Defining Moments: White Australia policy", National Museum of Australia, July 21, 2020. (online).
125 "The Battle of Broken Hill and repercussions for the German Community", *Migration Heritage Centre* (NSW Government), 2011. (online).
126 Rory Callinan, "Sydney siege: Man Haron Monis's flurry of letters revealed", *Sydney Morning Herald*, December 19, 2014. (online).
127 Matthew Thomas, "The 1967 Referendum", Parliament of Australia, May 25, 2017. (online).
128 Emma Reynolds, "Why NSW had most marginal Yes vote of any state", news.com.au, November 15, 2017. (online).
129 "How Well Did Pauline Hanson's One Nation Do In The 2016 Federal Election?", Australianpolitics.com, August 10, 2016. (online).
130 "Turnbull first PM to host iftar for Ramadan", Special Broadcasting Corporation, June 17, 2016. (online).
131 Paul Karp, "Malcolm Turnbull regrets inviting homophobic sheikh to Iftar dinner", *The Guardian*, June 17, 2016. (online).
132 Pallavi Thakur, "Why are non-Muslims not allowed in Mecca?", Speaking Tree, April 16, 2014. (online).
133 Emna Baccar, "The Christian Negus and the Stick: A Reflection as a Muslim at Mass", *Berkley Centre for Religion, Peace, & World Affairs* (Georgetown University), January 12, 2015. (online).
134 "Federal Protection of Freedom of Religion or Belief", Inquiry into the status of the human right to freedom of religion or belief (Parliament of Australia), November, 2017. (online).

BIBLIOGRAPHY

Books and Articles

Abbas, S. B., *Pakistan's blasphemy laws from Islamic empires to the Taliban*, University of Texas Press, 2014.

Adler, E. N., *Jewish travellers in the Middle Ages: 19 firsthand accounts*, Dover, 2016.

Aglionby, J. Indonesia's first woman president, *The Guardian*, July 26, 2001.

Al-Rasheed, M., Kersten, C., & Shterin, M. *Demystifying the Caliphate: Historical memory and contemporary contexts*, Oxford University Press, 2016.

Ali, S. M., *The position of women in Islam: A progressive view*, State University of New York Press, 2004.

Bennett, C, *Muslim women of power: Gender, politics, and culture in Islam*, Continuum, 2010.

Bhutto, B. Daughter of the East: An autobiography. Pocket Books, 2008.

Bouachrine, I., *Women and Islam: Myths, Apologies and the Limits of Feminist Critique.* Lexington Books, 2015.

Bowen, W. H., *The History of Saudi Arabia*, 2nd ed, 2015. ABC-CLIO, LLC.

Burger, J, Where are the oldest churches in Africa?, Aleteia (online), 29 March 2019.

Cooper, A. S, *Fall of Heaven: The Pahlavis and the Final Days of Imperial Iran.* Picador, 2018.

Callinan, R, Sydney Siege: Man Haron Monis' flurry of letters revealed, *Sydney Morning Herald*, 19 December 2014.

Commonwealth Parliament, & Parliament House, The 1967 Referendum, 25 May 2017.

Commonwealth Parliament & Parliament House, 4. Federal Protection of Freedom of Religion or Belief, 1 December, 2017.

Cook, S. A., *Laws of Moses and the code of Hammurabi*. Gaunt, 2013.

Duri, A. A., *The Historical Formation of the Arab Nation* (RLE: The Arab Nation). Routledge, 2012.

Esposito, J. L., *The Oxford History of Islam*, Oxford University Press, 2010.

Fatton, R. & Ramazani, R. K., *Future of Liberal Democracy Thomas Jefferson and the Contemporary World*. Palgrave Macmillan, 2004.

Gerli, E. M., *Medieval Iberia: An Encyclopedia*. Routledge, 2017.

Gil, M., *Jews in Islamic countries in the Middle Ages*. Brill, 2011.

Ghadanfar, M. A., *Great women of Islam: Who were given the good news of paradise*. Darussalam, 2001.

Hashim, A., Pakistan passes landmark transgender rights law, *Aljazeera*, 9 May 2018.

Hathaway, O. A., & Shapiro, S. J., Outlawing War? It Actually Worked, New York Times, 2 September 2017.

Hjelmgaard, K., Iran's Jewish community is the largest in the Mideast outside Israel – and feels safe and respected, *USA Today*, 1 September 2018.

Holt, P. M., Lambton, A. K., & Lewis, B., *The Cambridge history of Islam*, University Press, 1970.

Ilanbey, S., Towell, N., & Zhuang, Y., 'Completely abhorrent': Julia Banks slams former Liberal colleague Gladys Liu, *Sydney Morning Herald*, 16 April 2019.

Ingber, S., 70 Muslim Clerics Issue fatwah Against Violence And Terrorism, NPR, 11 May 2018.

Islam, M. N., *Pakistan and Malaysia: A Comparative Study in National Integration*. Sterling Pub, 1989.

Johnston, D. M. *Religion, Terror, and Error: U.S. Foreign Policy and the Challenge of Spiritual Engagement* (Praeger Security International). Praeger, 2011.

Karp, P., Malcolm Turnbull regrets inviting homophobic sheikh to Iftar dinner, *The Guardian*, 17 June 2016.

Mattson, I., Nesbitt-Larking, P., & Tahir, N., *Religion and representation: Islam and democracy*. Cambridge Scholars Publishing, 2015.

Millar, L., Women will wait 200 years for gender equality, Gillard says, ABC Online, 3 April 2018.

Mills, T., 'May their organs implode': How Melbourne teen Jake Bilardi was groomed by IS, *The Age*, 2 November 2017.

Moosa, E., & Kenney, J. T., *Islam in the modern world*. Routledge, 2014.

Queen Rania: A great role model, *The Jordan Times*, 14 June 2018.

Ratcliffe, R., FGM rates in east Africa drop from 71% to 8% in 20 years, study shows, *The Guardian*, 7 November 2018.

Sekulow, J., *Unholy Alliance: The Agenda Iran, Russia and Jihadists share for Conquering the World*. Simon & Schuster, 2017.

Sales, B., Exploring Ties Between Halacha and Shariah, *Forward*, 2 November 2011.

Sue Reid, 'You are now entering Sharia law Britain: As Islamic extremists declare a Sharia law zone in a London suburb, there are worrying social and moral implications', *The Mail on Sunday*, 29 July 2011.

Theodosiou, Peter, Jihad: A word which doesn't mean war against non-Muslims, SBS, 9 August 2016.

Whinnett, E., Australian Dr Jihad 'killed fighting for ISIS', *Adelaide Now*, 8 June 2018.

Worth, R. F., In Syrian Villages, the Language of Jesus Lives, *New York Times*, 22 April 2008.

Webpages

Al-Qur'an al-Kareem: https://quran.com

Berkley Center for Religion: https://berkleycenter.georgetown.edu

BibleGateway: https://www.biblegateway.com

Bible Hub: https://biblehub.com/

Bible Study Tours: https://www.biblestudytools.com

Encyclopaedia Britannica: https://www.britannica.com

Encyclopedia Judaica: https://www.jewishvirtuallibrary.org

Islam and Homosexuality: http://islamandhomosexuality.com/5-queer-muslims-history/

Letter to Baghdadi: http://lettertobaghdadi.com/

Migration Heritage: http://www.migrationheritage.nsw.gov.au

Muslims for Liberty: https://muslims4liberty.org/

My Jewish Learning: https://www.myjewishlearning.com

US History: http://www.ushistory.org

www.ingramcontent.com/pod-product-compliance
Lightning Source LLC
Chambersburg PA
CBHW051744230426
43670CB00012B/2159